I0437048

Mt. Hersey Road

Mt. Hersey Road

FINDING NATURE AFTER FIFTY YEARS

by

DOROTHY THURSTON

Copyright © 2012 by Dorothy Thurston

All rights reserved.

ISBN: 1479206342
ISBN 13: 9781479206346

Dedication

To the animals

Table of Contents

Preface xi

Acknowledgments xv

BOOK I: NEARING THE WOODS 1

Chapter 1 Back-Road Bound 3

Chapter 2 Thoughts from the Runoff 15

Chapter 3 Human and Animal Passersby 37

BOOK II WANDERINGS 65

Chapter 1 Heading Out 69

Chapter 2 Winding Down Summer 93

Chapter 3 Society of Nature 109

Conclusion 129

Preface

When I look back fifty years to 1962, I remember record players, movie theaters, pinball machines, live weekly shows on television, and talking on telephones, over which one could only hear and speak, not see or type messages. News was reported primarily by newspapers, radio, and TV. Travel by bus and train was still in vogue. The population of the United States was 126 million less than today. Personal computers were not yet born, and terrorism, violence, and global economic problems did not seem as obtrusive in everyday news as they are today. We were urged to make as much money as possible, marry well and have children, attend church functions, become leaders in the community, and gain status in society, much the same as today. We were supposed to gather the fruits of materialism as the symbols of our success. Nature was seldom mentioned in our goals. The year 1962 was uncomplicated compared to 2012, but in both times, woods, and the intangible rewards they offer, have remained relatively ignored as a way to personal fulfillment.

I was twenty-two in 1962. I regarded life as an uninspired routine concerning income, survival, and dependence on estab-lishmentarian conformity. From business to social life, religion, education, and everyday practicalities, I tried to compete and struggle, yet arrived at a sense of futility with the unanswered question, "Why?" Before that year was out, I let thoughts tum-ble into my notebooks, with the resulting manuscript *Wanderings* offering a palliative remedy for the materialistic and frivolous venue in which most of us struggled. The main plan was first and foremost for simplification, based on a realization that society needed nature, namely trees, as found in their natural state in unspoiled woods. But the demands of daily living soon took over and I put the manuscript in a drawer, where it lay for fifty years.

Fifty years older now in 2012, I have found the old papers and realize that the ideas they contain never left me. In some ways, I now conclude, my life since 1962 has been a waste without continuing toward something more meaningful amid the hoopla and convention of prevailing materialistic society. I support the idea that society needs nature now more than ever. While the world has changed markedly by growing even more materialistic and populated, I am the same person that I was at twenty-two with the ideas that I had then, only now modified to reflect the passage of time. As a reward for the metamorphosis of aging, I believe I deserve the privilege of placing *Nearing the Woods,* the conclusion completed in 2012, first as Book I. *Wanderings,* the earlier work, is placed as Book II, but not because I don't still give it credence.

Sometimes, in both books, I use the word *nature* with a small *n*, sometimes with a capitalized *N*. When I think *nature* represents a higher quality of self, I take the privilege of capitalizing the initial letter to form *Nature*, which I still seek and am finding. As for myself, I am simply one human, unidentified by name, an example of universal humanity.

On the day, on the very day, of my death
I saw all the things of nature very clearly.
I saw the sky with its red lines
Ever floating against the horizon.
I saw the wind, which whistled through me
The way it had always done.
I saw the ground brown and sturdy,
Always ready to reflect my leaning shadow.
I saw the grey round rocks on that ground;
They made crisp outlines against it.
And in the clearness of my vision

I realized, on this very episode of death,
That the child who first saw these things
Has not forgotten;
That these things have not moved since then;
That the affairs apart from these very basic things
Were a nothingness, a whirlwind, and a dissolution.

WESTERN GROVE, ARKANSAS
SUMMER 2012

Acknowledgments

I am grateful to Patricia Anderson, Ph.D., for her expert editing and advice, and to Kenneth T. "Terry" Reed, Ph.D., for his advice and encouragement.

BOOK I
Nearing the Woods

Back-Road Bound

What prompts ideas contrary to conventional thinking? Perhaps an individual or group does not feel accepted or feels unappreciated and rejected. If new ideas for coping by that individual or group help them feel better, life becomes more comfortable as alternate ways of being or living replace the political and business scenes and even the ways that people amuse themselves through entertainment and travel. The idea is to dispel the underlying emptiness or pain behind the activity in question. Maybe feelings of emptiness or futility can never be completely dispelled, especially in view of the finality of death, but some of us try to adapt our lifestyles. Some adopt nature, whatever it means to them.

Nature, as referred to here, loosely means woods, uncut and flourishing, with old and young trees on vast tracts that do not blatantly show boundary lines or the neighbors' homes or pastures. Yet *nature* in this country is often reduced to images of commercialized camping in huge metal homes on wheels, near groups of smiling people grilling over smokers in a park, or in that same park, ambient scenes of hunting the flesh of wild animals—alive and cute prior to the kill but not shown after the arrow or bullet has ruined them. Idealized photos of cleared farmland, sometimes described as back-to-the-land, hide the pens, steel equipment, brutal trucks of animal husbandry, and conveyor belts needed to sort the eggs and apples of farm production. Images of leisurely walking in wooded areas, without the mission of the kill or the distracting chatter of "nature walkers," are infrequent. Population grows along with technology, while the peaceful atmosphere of the woods, affording opportunity to think amorphously outside of society's well-worn expectations, becomes harder to find.

✳   ✳   ✳

In 1990 I came to this place in the Ozarks, near the town-remnant of Western Grove, Arkansas, population posted as 407 on a sign near the post office. I was weary of the relationships that had disappointed and the jobs that were only efforts to survive. I bought forty "wooded acres" at $525 an acre on the north side of Mt. Hersey Road, an unpaved road that winds five miles down from Highway 65 to the Buffalo National River, the nation's first national river, that by law of 1972 does not allow motorized boats and must maintain a natural buffer on each side without logging or building. A barbed wire fence left from the previous owner, a pig farmer, completely surrounded the square containing the forty acres, which were additionally secured by a steel gate, although it had been broken down several times by those who wished access for hunting. The gate was back on hinges when I looked the place over, and with its capacity to be padlocked, I hoped I could find the solitude and peace that this area seemed to promise. If the previous owner's house had not burned to the ground, I would not have this property today, as his home had tried to be modern in the days of old farmhouses, while I wanted a simple cabin. A drilled well remained which I recognized as potentially useful. The property had the additional attraction of being only a half mile from the river.

By coming to an uncluttered place, I considered myself to be scouting for the important kernel of life under the shell that surrounds it. In his 1845 book, *Walden*, the nature writer Henry David Thoreau described his wanting to "drive life into a corner" while, for only two years, living "deliberately" in and around a primitive cabin in a wood, at a time when woods were much more available. What is in the essential kernel of life that can be communicated? After residing here for twenty-two years, I've concluded that the kernel must be felt by an individual and cannot be transplanted in complete affect to another. It cannot be verbalized in totality; it can be communicated only minimally. That is why I will seem to be circling, ever circling, around the feelings I really want to record and perhaps communicate in words, but never quite landing at the effective transmission. I can't feel for anyone but myself; I can't expect another to exactly experience my thoughts. I have often wondered if I am really just one person or mind dreaming that others exist. I think I know better, but since I have never lived in the head of another person or animal, it does seem logical to wonder if I am the only "I" really available. But such thinking goes nowhere.

I liked this specific property because no one had recently settled on it. There were just a few signs of the fire of years ago in blackened glass shards and half-melted plastic pipes. A rickety chicken coop, smokehouse, and pigpen were all that were still standing within a quarter of a mile. It was not much land by the standards of the previous few centuries, but it seemed adequate. It bothered me a bit that exactly a quarter of a mile away, next door, a house had been built and was occupied currently. Fortunately, I can hear the occupant only when the man fires his gun in practice for hunting season, although out of sight of the road, and I can't see him or his family through my woods at all. I wanted aloneness, to be alone, to be stark against the landscape, but to feel only minimally lonely. I wanted my simple place to blend discreetly and unobtrusively with the environment and with no peeking neighbors. Indeed, I wanted to appear invisible to anyone traversing the road nearby.

It is not with other people that I want to find myself; I seek what remains after the other people are out of sight and mind. Of course, it is impossible to divorce myself completely from the knowledge or awareness of other people, but nature is more attractive if one sees it with no one in view. Who wants a picture of a person standing against a wooded backdrop? Perhaps the person's relatives would, but I would not want to grace the walls of ultimate thoughts with it. I want to see the vistas without bodies present, including my own. I can meet myself there through my own thoughts against the unobstructed view of Nature in a better way than when I have to pose with people that I must try to impress, say the polite thing, dwell upon human inconsequentiality, or arrange my hair and smile appropriately.

I intended to leave behind the everyday world of work in towns, to attempt to build and occupy a primitive cabin that I would have someone construct for pay. The former landowner told me that the property had not been molested by loggers in forty years—"a forty-year growth"—and with exception of the cleared area closest to the fence, where the owner's home once stood, I did not see overt signs of logging on the road for half a mile, at least. Today, in 2012, my property comprises more than a sixty-year growth, as I have been here these twenty-two years. It seems like moments ago that I moved here; I still feel like a newcomer. Yet during my residence, properties near here have been partially logged, and people have come and gone. Only in the past six or seven years have I really been able to appreciate the property that I own and protect. So many trees are now completely mature and lush. Some places are overgrown, and my privacy is a hard-won prize as part of a forest of comfort and peace.

The only human noises occurring now on a semi-regular basis are from the unpaved road, unseen from my cabin, on which vans and trucks carry canoes and people to the river. One may also hear the yelps of children on ATVs and the voices of the agricultural populace who frequently stop on the road on their tractors to discuss cropping, family, and weather with others.

County road graders are heard clashing and scraping, but these graders keep the road intact after washouts.

Four hundred feet of dirt driveway proceed up to my little hill from the gate, which stands ready to lock me into this natural haven and to lock out understandably curious persons who may want to see the hermit who resides here. For most of my occupancy I've kept a lock on this gate, locking myself in and the world out, but around five weeks ago, I briefly removed the lock for my own ease of entry, still wrapping the chain around the latch. It seems I'm not as unique as I thought I was: no one opened the gate to enter to see the oddball within. To really come into my world, however, would be to open more than a steel gate. My real gate is actually penetrable, with or without a lock, but requires more subtle access.

These original forty acres bordered U.S. Government land to the south when I took possession. I didn't think too much about this then, but around 1993, I heard the Buffalo National River surveyors calling to each other within earshot of my cabin, and I was most pleased to learn that the First National River had acquired this land behind me to add to its holdings, thus assuring no logging or building could assault my senses from the back. Clearly, my property fit the well-worn description "diamond in the rough."

The previous owners were homeless after their 1980 fire, but they had somehow dragged two very old "tourist cabins" from the bank of the river up the road to their property for use as shelter until they could rebuild their home. But the couple gave up the struggle to rebuild and moved to another state, where they remained eight years before I spotted their property for sale. The ancient and dilapidated tourist cabins were here when I took over. After acquiring the deed to the acreage, I hired two men who used heavy equipment to drag these structures up to a little space behind a treed bluff, an area not visible from the road. I had them placed enough apart to allow for a kitchen to be built between them out of new materials. The two outer rooms are now the original tourist cabins, saved for the charm of their unique walls and ceilings of narrow plywood, although the floors were noticeably weak in areas. The whole structure of my "new" cabin became three rooms totaling 900 square feet, with the tiny rooms connected by interior doors. A new board-and-batten wood exterior is the mask that hides the pathetic crudeness of the entire structure, but simplicity and charm show both inside and out. I later applied wood stain to both the exterior and parts of the interior, and windows were made for seven openings. A wood-burning stove, gas stove, and gas refrigerator were installed along with the inevitable outside propane tank.

An old-fashioned tub with claw feet was brought in. Two sinks complete the indoor plumbing fixtures. The water is pumped uphill from the well-house 200 feet away. Within this tiny well-house is a specially designed pump powered by a car battery that in turn is charged by a solar panel. Low-flow water is thus supplied to the cabin in narrow pipes but not without freezing problems in winter. Two other solar panels stationed on the ground provide for a radio and minimal lighting inside; my reading lamp is a five-watt bulb on a wand over the bed in the main room. The know-how on solar power was provided by a small company in Kingston, Arkansas.

I had a metal chimney inserted into the cabin roof. The chimney connects downward through the main room to the heavy iron wood-burning stove, made in Yellville, Arkansas, and bought at Miller's Hardware in Harrison, twenty miles away. I never had experience starting a fire using just firewood and kindling, and I had much to learn regarding the use of paper kindling, wood kindling, starter pieces made with grease and wax, and kerosene spray. I needed patience to get a fire going that would not fade after five minutes. I often keep a winter coat on for several hours while warming up the main room that contains the bed. After a few hours, the main room usually becomes cozy enough for the kind of sleep that really provides peace and repair. Keeping the heat confined to one room speeds the process of warming to a comfortable temperature to within two hours, but this is still an ungodly amount of time in single-digit temperatures.

Even without electricity and the technology of 2012 — including email, which allows people to communicate minimally, although not face-to-face—my cabin, when finally heated, provides a warm and inviting place to read, rest, and perhaps concentrate on writing if the heat stays relatively constant. I have all the basic comforts that I need and have long since finished with my early activity of accumulating clothing, pans, table, bed, blankets, shelves, chairs, and a radio for weather reports. The complete privacy, in locked-in isolation, removes my former concern about the possible curiosity of human eyes that might peer at me as an oddity in my restorative place. Now, at last, I can sit and rest and read, surrounded by desirable forms of nature, including runoff streams, trees, rocks, and small moving creatures—raccoons, possums, groundhogs, and occasional armadillos. But almost all of the foxes and coyotes that were here in 1990 have been killed by hunters.

The original forty acres and the materials, including solar panels and labor for the completed structure, came to around $46,000 in 1990. The name of the cabin is Woodscape, but this is not very imaginative; I've seen a brand of paint with the same name.

✳　✳　✳

Before a lasting contentment could come from my living here, I had to deal with the earsplitting sounds of the distant chainsaws, skidders, and bulldozers of the ubiquitous loggers. My sensibilities, interpreting these as signals of approaching danger and insult, made me aware that I was not yet "out of the woods," a poor expression since where I wanted to be was, in fact, *in* the woods. I soon realized how much out of woods I could easily become, given that in 1997 my cabin sat within yards of the boundary line, sealing me in on the east side from the adjacent forty acres of trees, probably seventy years old. People often look at land as potential logging sites, and should I grow lazy and inattentive, I could find myself overlooking a dump of stumps, paragons of simplicity lost. Indeed, in 1997, I found the land east of the line was about to be ravaged by a logger-profiteer who made his living buying inexpensive large parcels from people, some of whom lived out-of-state. He would log off all the marketable wood, then sell the devastated property at an escalated price to those who don't mind broken woods. Logging this way is a profitable living but one I would not have the heart myself to pursue. The young logger had recently purchased the land from a woman in Illinois whose father had owned it in the 1930s. Logging was to begin without delay.

After high-pitched words of negotiations with the logger and his mother, I managed to purchase this tract from him for $29,400, which I borrowed, bringing him a considerable profit and preventing the cutting from beginning. In the negotiations, however, the property's legal description had been worded in a way that meant I would have been legal owner of only half of what I thought I was buying. To straighten this out, I was obliged to run an ad several times in the local newspaper, inviting any persons of the past, going back to the late 1800s, who might have any claim to ownership with the correct description, to make their voices heard. I was successful in receiving no claims to dispute ownership, and I became the relieved owner of the forty-one acres to the east. It is a wondrous place where, from the looks of it, I assume that no logging has occurred for decades.

The next affront to my wooded retreat occurred in 1998 when the forty acres directly north of my original "forty" came up for sale across the road. A "For Sale" sign appeared and stayed for eight months. To have someone move there would have decimated my plans for peace and harmony, since the property contained only one building site south of its runoff creek, and this site gawks at my gate just a few feet away across the road. Indeed, a Fourth of July celebration took place there that year with every noise carrying clearly to my ears nearby, unbeknownst to the partyers. Unable to endure the worry that my haven would be permanently noise infested, I finally accepted an outright gift of $24,100 from a dear relative to pay off the owner. My cocoon now consisted of 120 acres, give or take a little, with my cabin centrally located.

I wasn't finished with my pursuit of quietude. An eighteen-acre strip, located south of the forty-one acres that I had purchased from the would-be logger, became my next concern. This strip, owned by a widow in Louisiana in 2003, was really a bluff on which rested the remains of the old "hippie shack," so-called by a farmer. The old shack of thirty years ago was once used by carefree youth for little parties, he said. The youth had built a roof over some wooden posts, calling it their home for a summer. They bathed, I heard, in the Buffalo River, and probably had fun in their summer-filled bedroom at night, telling wild stories over food and drink. The bluff would have been a likely place for an entrepreneur to build a house to be accessed by a road, which would have to be constructed from the back, east of the Buffalo River land. To prevent such near invasion, I badly needed to own this property. The far side of the bluff was a natural place to separate ownership.

After countless dead-end calls, I owe my success in locating the woman to one unknown man in Louisiana who generously gave me the information as to whom I needed to call. She was relieved to unload the burden of the eighteen acres that had been her husband's idea. I soon bought the land from her for $18,000, the last of my liquid funds, an amount that was her original purchase price. This made the final addition to my now complete 138-acre retreat. My land at Woodscape includes the three squares of approximately 40 acres each and the flanking strip of eighteen acres. Of course, the public dirt road runs through part of my land, but there are many quiet hours when no cars, trucks, road equipment, or people on horses are present.

The total cost for the 138 acres and cabin was around $118,000. I have to pause here to consider how lucky, while vigilant, I have been to arrive at this modicum of assured sanity in land ownership and preservation. In 2012, having such a natural retreat is not only desirable, but it is also unusual.

✳   ✳   ✳

Part of road maintenance is accomplished by the county graders, huge vehicular machines with plows attached. Having never seen or heard a grader before coming to the Ozarks, my first idea was that they were used infrequently in emergencies. I soon found that, as part of the services for which taxes are paid, counties send these and other machines on a scheduled, frequent, and regular basis to level and maintain unpaved roads. Scars left on trees unfortunate enough to grow by the sides of such roads are sometimes caused by the graders and other machines with screaming saws applied squarely in the middle of trunks or by long knives hoisted up to cut, tear, or shred. The roads seem to be getting wider every year as one-lane roadways are slowly becoming two lanes. I cringe every time I see (or more likely hear) these monsters coming down the road, and I sometimes escape in my car for town at these times. It is the same with the killing sounds of logging which, even at a distance, continue to attack my senses. I find I can no more tolerate the sounds now than I did when I first came here.

Every five years, the electric company sends its array of trucks, elevated saws, and torture devices looking for its overhead electric lines to defend and protect by clearing a broad swath of land under them. The huge bush-hog machines crisscross people's land relentlessly. Although I don't have electricity, they have cut the tops off some of my pretty trees, left vegetative carnage for me to clean up, sprayed poisonous chemicals on vegetation, and devalued the privacy and dignity of land and owner alike. The company even puts its locks on some people's gates. The private owner cannot easily voice objection.

There was the burying of telephone lines on my road for five miles, which took months to accomplish, with much equipment, digging, and pounding. There were also the water lines, to which I did not hook up, which also took months of heavy labor and equipment to install along Mt. Hersey Road from the town well five miles away. Failing to obtain my permission to have these lines buried on my property, to spoil the naturalness by killing many of the trees, the workers silently moved across the street, not bothering to ask permission of the then-owner. Later, I myself became the owner, but the part of the property which was affected by the underground pipe installation had been a pasture years before and did not appear to have overly suffered from tree killing at the hands of the water utility.

As for gushing springs, I can sympathize with those city- and suburb-weary people who come to a place still mostly removed from commercial victimization, thinking that year-round creeks, ponds, springs, and wild, never-logged countryside exist outside the madness of their society. An all-weather spring! What a pure and delicious sound! More than likely, however, a seeker of a bucolic state of nature, complete with a chaste all-weather spring, will be informed that such properties are no longer to be had. Either they are already in someone's possession, perhaps guarded aggressively from visitors who would trespass, or the pleasant old waters have mostly dried up. Perhaps they have been built over, have sunk back into a deeper part of the ground, or have been permanently hidden behind the fences of their keepers. Unless one is willing to put in months, years, and/ or significant money in searching for and buying such a treasure, the usual solution is to settle for a seasonal spring or a runoff creek, which may be active only some days of the year after a rain or snow melt. Sometimes a dried-up spring can be revived if one is willing to devote time and resources to a monstrous digging project. I don't believe leaders in public life would like it here. They are too accomplished in the world of people, too used to seeing many faces on a polite basis, and not used to digging out hidden springs.

I am here to take a break from the concrete world of necessity—of people, money, and things. Here I am able to enter into a comfortable mission of darks and lights, reveries hidden in the shades of tans and greens, quiet beatitude among fluttering leaves. At least I have a cabin within parcels of trees, even if I can't belong to a whole society with such treasures in view.

CHAPTER 2

Thoughts from the Runoff

Might an individual stand alone part of the time to determine the essential core of his life? In the nineteenth century, Thoreau tried to answer this question by moving to his cabin in the woods to "suck out all the marrow of life," the core that is left after dealing with other people and things. His book *Walden* seems marvelously erudite in describing the conditions of the land, his cabin, the few neighbors, and nearby plant and animal life. His isolated lifestyle helped him break from some pretentious and hypocritical aspects of society while his feelings of peace and tranquility intermingled with the hard work of hoeing beans and making a chimney.

Thoreau's was a noble effort but I wonder if he allowed that his basic goal was not entirely accomplished. Thoreau could not absent himself totally from the world and the town, and he still needed to socialize with the people that were his present and past. We cannot divorce ourselves from the sensory world we've lived in or are impressed by. There is no person who relates to a void.

The three-dimensional field is ours and we interpret that field in our unique ways. Nevertheless, I feel I've joined Thoreau's efforts to see what remains while living on a relatively average patch of land that could still pass as "woods" today. To find woods now is not easy. The world is losing more and more of nature, the woods that parallel the unmolested core of ourselves, the solitude that holds the opportunity for contemplation. But contemplation of what?

I still think like I did a long time ago. My surroundings are becoming a definition of myself. There is no such person called by my name that is somewhere other than where I live. By coming here, I have actually hidden myself from time-wasting activities and organizations. My fragility could not manage the exposure to the faces and criticism from the members. My opinions about things are too different, too moral sounding and solitary, to carry weight over the loud voices around me. The intense, rude, and noxious rantings of the conventionally energetic would kill the delicate life of silence. Perhaps there are others, quiet and detached like myself, who choose to remain in the more comfortable nest of privacy.

I have ample opportunity to observe the trees that, having been saved from logging, are the only views to the front, back, and sides of Woodscape. They are pleasantly stuck forever in the very places where they seeded and grew. Without faces, without brains as we know them, they live here and seem to like it. Apparently, trees form from a tangle of roots that quickly occupy the space below ground to send sprouts above to develop into trees eventually. Where in each tree is the central intelligence that feels, decides, and maybe even communicates? It would seem to be in the roots, ruminating in privacy below. But without eyes to see above their soil blanket, how can they determine where or when a stem should emerge? Without brains like those of humans, the roots survey the underground and make "decisions" to push up their newborn! This seems odd to me, but I am not a plant with roots in the ground! What about DNA in plants? Where are the genes and chromosomes located in each plant, and do they reveal, among other things, parental contribution?

Blackberry bushes send root probes from below to result in new foliage above, thorns and berries at distances many feet away from their starting places. I can't help but think that roots suffer anguish when someone is tampering with the branches above. Not having a real brain, do they experience pain if a trimmer cuts back their limbs? I am impressed with the overwhelming numbers of trees now on my land that were not in evidence when I came here.

✶   ✶   ✶

Sometimes I would have rather lived in the 1800s. There wasn't electricity then, but there wasn't the ugliness we see now. Thoreau complained about the newly appearing trains upsetting the tranquility of his paradise and about the cutting of trees by lumbermen. If alive today, Thoreau might be a different person, perhaps locked into a professorship with or without tenure at a university, advocating environmental consciousness. I don't think he could find much respect from today's world if he primarily lived in a cabin among trees, providing he could even find and afford some acreage of undisturbed woods on which to build it. He would probably be ostracized as "unsuccessful" or even sexually perverted. We have put nature on a back shelf, dragging it out as a harmless diversion. There possibly could be less room for him today to write a book like *Walden* or to appreciate nature; he might be quickly eliminated from serious consideration. Today he would have to deal with the products and concepts in an even more confusing world of material things and political maneuverings. Perhaps, today, "nature" has been reduced to streets lined with a few trees behind the nearest convenience store. We could visit those few trees after a foray to a store selling food, largely processed, and gadgets galore.

My cabin experience is hardly truly primitive. I drive to a superstore twice a month, taking up the good part of consciousness each day I make the trip. The day becomes the list I take with me to name this oil-based paint or that processed cheese, not to mention nails, fence posts, and batteries. But I am proud of this cabin, the residue of Thoreau's spirit, which enables me to have a modicum of satisfaction in living, after many years of failing to assimilate well among the herds. This account, therefore, is concerned more with the cabin experience than the things I do occasionally in town, which could label me "normal" when I need that designation for one reason or another.

Except for the noxious sounds of the distant loggers and nearby road machines — all of which are disruptive — there are not too many interruptions, and the fence keeps out the majority of curious parties. I can thus read off and on for hours, devouring at will the lessons from the philosophies of nonfiction, chosen to quietly consider their far-reaching and important applications in my own time. Reading and napping in a remote cabin when one is living alone can be very peaceful as long as I restrict the appointments I must keep or the rides to town I have promised. I am at liberty to relax and experience the sleep of the gods. Toward the end of the year when the seasons change, I can rest quite pleasantly in a place unlike any I have known before, on a bed wondrously endowed with many pillows, each contained in a different colored case for decoration, and as many blankets as I want for comfort. Especially when a wood fire is burning in the stove — with no other person to object to the amount of heat I want to build — does the bed, occupying the living room area, feel utterly luxurious. There are no distractions or "suggestions" from other people and no electronic time killers to keep me alert. Occasionally a cat will sleep with me; sometimes she is in the way when I change positions, but her warm fur blends with the soothing ambiance of the surroundings.

I don't grow anything for food here. Fortunately, a hermit up the road, who truly lives every day in a primitive condition without utilities of any kind, gives me plenty of greens during much of the summer: kale, lamb's quarters, watercress, mustard, and collard. I never make any big effort in cooking a meal; six small meals a day do the job, with the emphasis on "small." Currently, four out of the six meals are the same thing: a milk product with pudding. I eat like a queen, being careful to avoid fats and sugar as much as possible. I admire anyone who can eat sensibly without constant attendance to nutritional values, shopping, and preparing special "dishes." I do eat fish from cans, but I would prefer to be a total vegetarian. Whenever I eat the flesh of a creature once alive, whose body I add to my own, I am super-conscious that this was a being, however lowly, which perhaps had goals and unique ambitions and certainly an inborn tendency to continue being itself, a creature with or without a recognizable face, with hopes and fears, for the most part. Why were we made to eat other creatures is one of the questions I ask myself when considering the purpose and fairness of creation.

By living simply in the center of 138 acres, wooded and uncut for decades, I have in effect gained thousands of square feet of living space. My little home exceeds its tiny enclosure. I have rooms and rooms outside and a small building inside! My house extends outward, bounded only by the walls of thick foliage. I have a mansion of nature. No one sees me if I walk in rooms within a green protective curtain. My trees allow me to expand walls until they almost reach the wire fence by the road. There someone could peer through the fence and see me, were I nearby. I am wealthier than the homeowners who paid many thousands of dollars for great houses with their dooryards of mowed house lots. It is hard to believe that, in 2012, I am owner of a cabin with so many unaltered tree companions, while elsewhere the woodlands will no doubt continue to evaporate. I'm glad my life was not programmed for hundreds of years from now to confront advanced devastation.

If I were to look down from a plane today, I suppose I would see what would still appear to be countryside galore even with our country's population of 312 million, which actually is much less than some countries have. It appears we could have all the beauteous land we could hope for, but to reach any of it in person, one has to first travel on a road. Roads enter land that is being developed or populated, but to get to real natural beauty, one would need to exit a public road, and this would mean entering someone's private property. Primarily, landowners have the only real access to remote land, and I surmise this was also true in Thoreau's day, although then there were fewer people and they owned greater tracts of land. Today, as more and more people are pushing to own tracts of beautiful land, they could find them unaffordable, unavailable, reduced in size, or vigorously defended by present holders of title.

✻   ✻   ✻

There is the lawn game that many of society's homeowners play. Get out a push mower, riding mower, tractor, bush-hog machine, or weed-eater at every available hour every week from around April through October. Get to pruning, mowing, or weeding or you won't have a setup like the neighbor's lawn, which is deliberately in public view and evaluated by precision of manicure, cost of the decorative plants, and depth of their colors. For myself, I have no lawn. I abide by the caveat, "Lose the lawn." How much prettier is a natural front and back view of maturing natural growth with wild animals sometimes seen! It is not so much the building or structure that is important but the land where the place rests. Instead of having one's lawn go all the way back from the road, why not have just a few feet of clearance at the entrance to the property, leaving the rest of it natural, allowing for the thinnest band of "driveway"? Of course, someone moving into suburban America where all the yards are mowed right up to each naked building would understandably be hesitant to risk his reputation as a clean and orderly citizen, were he to let his property, be it one-third or three-fifths of an acre, grow up and out. If he wants freedom, it would probably be better for him to resist moving to a neighborhood where the pressures to conform are rampant.

Before now, when I lived on streets packed with small homes, my regular dealings with the faces of other humans usually tripped an internal siren warning me to conclude the business with them as soon as possible and find a solitary nook offering quiet comfort. I devise more decisions of significance when I am alone than when I deal with faces up close. Now without the daily faces, I do not feel empty or deprived, but just the opposite, and rarely am I lonely in my isolation. I have matters of importance in my brain and enough trees to stir my thoughts.

It seems to me that the kernel of life, the ultimate "meaning," is really an approach into an almost dreamlike quality of color, cloud, and vague melody that reverberates as the high ground without further ado. It does not preach, dictate, or recommend action. It swarms near a goal, but is not an arrow to people, stated purpose, things, governments, religious dictates, or parole cards. It tries to stay in the Now, but of course cannot stay for long. It seems to me it should be rather pleasant, for should not a goal for living approach contentment? What I seek, I think, is a direction bringing me a positive feeling of my universe, but I can't recognize anything for sure. It's merely a direction, and life continues from there. Some who call themselves artists occasionally seem to feel wondrous moments, whether or not these moments are captured in a "work." Such moments for them are most likely elevating and private and not necessarily the same for all: each vision is constructed according to what brings positive wonder to an individual before and after the world of people and practical matters. It seems to me that each person should be his own artist.

During history, many art objects, including paintings and sculpture, have been praised as masterful. Personally, I have identified with certain paintings hanging in overnight lodges and motels, possibly created by unknown persons specifically hired to relay a sense of quietude and peace in rooms for rent. The sense of ultimate peace I have felt in a room with such adornment apparently is similarly felt by others; it is a feeling related to a non-conceptualized world, such as nature. I could identify with a simple statement by an unknown expressing feelings about winter, summer, spring, or fall–removed from the concepts, definitions, and outlines of mundane commerce—bringing the colors, shapes, light, and humble suggestions of nature's seasons and man's. Yet the "masters" of antiquity or even of this age are often acclaimed for their superbly "realistic" and meticulous rendering of street life and scenery, for exactitude of likeness to leaders or events in history, or for illustrations of gatherings seated at holiday tables in the halls of yesterday or in contemporary dining rooms. But mundane commerce and conviviality are not the reality of myself. I would congratulate an unknown artist who speaks to me in paintings that seem to evoke the kind of rest I welcome on a trip, or in life. What I really seek, however, is a bit more than the contentment portrayed in motel-room paintings. But it is a start and, in my opinion, supercedes the importance of most galleried and juried paintings in great museums.

Occasionally, like the exchange through certain motel room paintings, an avenue of new awareness comes after meeting another person who becomes unknowingly responsible for raising feelings of wonder. The extent of the influence may not be verbalized or even recognized at the time. It may come after a few acquainting encounters when meeting in the street or in a classroom. This kind of relationship may occur rarely, and resulting awareness may be carried to Nature for further processing.

It is difficult to get out of society. Most of us have to drive vehicles; I had to drive one just to find a patch of woods for sale; walking here from another state would have been unworkable. I still have to go to town for necessities, even though I am fortunate now not to have to work there for endless hours just to maintain my right to exist. A life before motorized vehicles and electronic networking surely leant itself to more uninterrupted private time when individuals had to rely on themselves. Today, one is tagged as deviant if reclusive behavior is evident. Even on a back-road, it is hard for one to escape public opinion, encroachment of construction, endless gadgets of electronic communication, and political and religious pressures. Each person is subject to concepts of social conformity, although they can be less evident out here.

I want to keep looking and moving until I find or make happen what is primarily important to me, even if I have to lose my social status, if any, in the process. What have I got if I don't try? I have wanted a place in the woods all my life with the original hope of getting there in the company of another person (with whom I have not yet made acquaintance). I think perhaps just being here by myself is what I really sought, even though I did not accept being alone in this mission for years before I came here. Of course, there are sacrifices attached to any decision: you have to give up something to get anything. Thus I have gained much by being here on my own.

✧   ✧   ✧

From the river's edge where I occasionally walk, the water seems to move as one unit, occasionally splashing, spraying, and gurgling over rocks. It sings optimistically as an entity to any bystander that reckons with it, even crosses it. Scoop up a handful of water from the moving dynamo and let a drop fall out of your hand, or let fall a handful, half a handful maybe. The river then is not a body at all; it is just a bunch of wiggly wet parts that have found each other but which are not even glued together. I am mostly like the river; I identify with its continually moving down the path prepared for it. It moves and doesn't appear to stop and doesn't even falter when it reaches its first hurdle. It joins another moving hulk of water, but some of it gushes out into the river's sides. Occasionally, I would like the river of my life to stop, to hold onto the fun and satisfaction or the mysterious and mystical glee. But I myself can't stop it, and parts of myself break off and evaporate in the tiny rivulets from the sides. I can think I know when it will stop, however. My happiness and my sorrow continue passing, only moving by and with me. My big goal had been to reach a permanent station of joy. I now realize that I will never reach such permanence. I'll just glean what I can as the river moves on.

I consider fire. After an hour or so, I can usually get an adequate fire burning in my wood-burning stove. Sometimes I have to throw in a bit of water through the opened door if it gets too rambunctious. I still have a persistent fear that when I absent the cabin for any reason, the smoldering ashes could escape to the outside of the stove or burn a hole through the thin steel chimney, then move to the original and deteriorating floor of my living room. That would be fire working as a unit of destruction. Are there fire atoms? What is fire anyway? It must have different atoms from those of a river. Has anyone seen a water atom before it evaporates? Sometimes a roaring fire in my wood-burning stove seems noisier than a raging Buffalo River, which flows at the turnoff down the road.

There is more water afoot! Is it really true that one can dig a hole and eventually reach water almost anywhere? I have a 125-foot well from which water is brought to surface by a twelve-volt submersible pump. I know there are places one must dig much deeper to discover water under the land. I wonder how long my well water segued below the earthy crust just waiting to seep deeper within or to come aboard ground-top for the thirsty purposes of my needs.

All of this is a bit confusing. Does all land actually rest on water? Or water on land? The tectonic plates of land, said to bump into each other at times, supposedly can cause earthquakes and tsunamis from the chaos and upheavals beneath the seas and land. What do the lands of the ocean floor rest on? Fire? More water farther down? I've heard that the center of the earth is a molten core. Surely this is the final resting place of all the seas, land, and trickles of water above.

I believe I have arrived as a person whose outer trappings reflect my inner world. Here I am free to think anything I want—about ultimate purposes, joys, sad partings—and to conjure up interpretations to place with these thoughts. I am free to imbue recollected events and feelings with meaning that is right for me. These thoughts are myself in their forming. The unrestricted greenery outside my cabin door each morning is what I have been leaning toward since the time I began to really think and ruminate. Without this retreat, without a deliberate move to live alone in Nature, I could have only suspected that there was something I didn't do, something I missed. This is a setting that offers continuous opportunity to consider Thoreau's constantly moving stream of time that he went "a-fishing in." I can be alive listening to the sounds of small wild animals creeping, trees sweeping, and the darkness of the evening. I can leave the windows uncovered and not fear the eyes of mischievous adults or children. No one sees me. I am completely enclosed by green canopy. I can be my own company, entertaining myself with my thoughts and not really feeling alone. To think about the alternative as a restricted pawn in a social network would be tiring and unnecessary.

I can see the stars at night. From here, anyone who could not see them must be blind or fading. Is this a joke or am I in a trance? Are there really stars or physical properties out there where the lights appear to originate? It is said we see the delayed light coming from light-years away. I wonder if I were to follow a line of light backwards from here with the purpose of reaching the source of the light, which scientists say turned on eons ago, would I really arrive at the source, since the light would stop a bit before the source? Isn't the light moving away from it and possibly retreating and disappearing from the source? Would I meet the source anyway if I were to somehow continue backward toward it? Even if I could no longer see the light? Shouldn't dust particles be there to reflect the light? Can the line of light move from the present to the past without a gap?

It would seem that we here on Earth should not only see the old beams up there at night but should occasionally see a beam actually make a spotlight on the ground where I stand, if the beam has truly arrived on our planet—a spotlight such as one would see if a high-intensity flashlight were aimed from a tree to the ground. If I floated in space looking up close at the light that originated from a star, providing that there were dust particles for the light to bounce against (which may not exist), would the light appear to move zip-zip as it flies away from the originator? I hear some originator stars have long since disappeared, or imploded or exploded to complete the scenario, but their light moves on. On the other hand, perhaps light does not just travel in a line like a highway through the desert, but just diffuses outward away from the source, eventually striking everything within viewing distance. If one sees the starlight, I wonder if it has arrived or if it is still moving toward us in an overall diffusion and if I would know when the light has actually arrived here. After arriving, with no more light to come, will it swallow itself up, the end of the light being greedily devoured by the soil here as it burns out like a candlewick, only faster?

If I were to go floating in space billions of miles from anybody or anything pulling on me, I wonder if I would just hang there without moving, or by flapping my arms and legs manage to gain a few feet here and there. While suspended up there, I wonder if I would occasionally see objects lighting up one by one as light arrives on them from a star. Well, I know when our sun's light has arrived on Earth because it lights up the sky. I guess I can be thankful for that.

I have always wondered what would happen if an imaginary spaceship reached the end of the universe or of all universes. Would it hit a transparent wall saying, "Private; do not enter"? Somehow it seems that where I was before birth is what awaits me on the other side of that sign. Just before I might get to the sign, I hope I would still have enough mind-presence to politely hold the door for someone of lesser strength. The thing I would not want to do is to be a demanding and totally egregious grouch at that time.

More astounding when I think of it is that a certain one of the single-celled organisms, which are said by scientists to be primitive Earth's initial life forms 3 to 4 billion years ago, must have been on a certain rock or water body at a certain time. This single cell must have self-divided into multi-celled forms, eventually requiring mates to produce the organisms that are here now. Without the particular single-celled organism that started my chain, I would never have come to be. My life, therefore, depends and depended on every move my predecessors made, from the beginning of life on Earth through every shade and nuance of environmental influence over the eons. One of my ancient grandmothers could have been a simple bit, not even that sexual, which rested on a pebble in the Baltic, if the Baltic had a shape then, at a temperature far above anything I as a human could endure. It's not just that my mother came from a farm in Missouri. It's what a single-celled organism was and did, how it interacted with like forms, and how its progeny adapted over time to changes taking place in its world. This is not even to mention the overall course of infinity, with its various moods, which brought about the world and the organism in the first place. But for now, I think I descended from one particular primitive cell, and this could be my greatest grandmother.

☆   ☆   ☆

Over the past twenty-two years, I have adopted eleven cats that people have dumped within an easy catwalk to my house: Jiggs, Wimp, Sloth, Patrick, Wild Thing, Whitey, Orange Cat, White Bibb, Bruder (died at approximately one year), Ragamuffin, and Fluffy. The latest cat that I "have" I've named Biggon since he's such a big one. Biggon has been coming over to get food, even though the neighbors think he's their cat, and I haven't included him as one of the eleven cats I've "adopted." I share what I have with all of them. Now just Fluffy and Biggon remain. They have their own flexible flap through a window to the inside of the cabin, but occasionally this flap becomes enticing to raccoons and possums, which is not to my liking. A person being lovable toward animals does not keep pets or farm animals outdoors or indoors all the time, lock birds in cages, or willingly kill fish with hooks and animals with guns, traps, or knives.

Fluffy has proved especially fond of sleeping with me, and her loud purring helps me at times to entertain sweet dreams. Upon the death of nine of these cats since 1990, I put them in bags and placed them under a certain tree, out of sight. Within two months the bags and bodies were gone, probably devoured or dispersed by wild animals or dogs who needed food badly. I don't have the courage to look at the spot under the tree before each animal's ascension allowance of two months.

☆   ☆   ☆

It seems that a person who is about to die has already done so in successive degrees: a confusion of personal finances and day-to-day organization, then memory loss, pain, or weakness of physical structure. Before death's moment, I surmise meaningful consciousness has already vanished and the person has slipped into the abyss in degrees without his own realization. My greatest concern is what it must be like to stop breathing, or in drowning, what it must be like to have water fill your lungs. It appears that, in the majority of instances, we are not aware of our final breaths, but I can't speak for a drowning person. The fear of death would seem to take place while feeling well or mostly cognizant. That is the time of the worst fear, I hope. The time of actual ceasing to be would simply be like walking a few steps in a fog (which have been walked over and over again earlier in the mind's imagery) and enduring the final blow, which we do not experience since we would hardly be conscious anyway. Much like the way a visit to the doctor that has been a source of worry for weeks ends up really being only a few physical steps into the office of the physician to receive the fast-paced treatment after the pain medicine is ingested. The endless pre-game which has already been played non-stop with great anguish, is worse than the actual fact, due to the difference in length of worry time. My long-feared death, I think, is right now as I worry about the "later."

I sometimes lie for hours with soft blankets and soft cat comforting me, affording the supreme opportunity to read, think, and nap. This is also when I feel more significance about the passage of long years, more likely now viewed as fleeting and short. I do not dwell on who died yesterday but on the fact of death itself. There certainly appears to me to loom ahead the disarrangement of my earthly form. If I were like an animal, supposedly unable to sense its imminent demise, I could probably live quite unaffected to the end. I must finally take the fact of death seriously. I await it in luxurious comfort often while resting, often with pad and pencil as well as book and cat. Some wild animals when held captive by humans often live longer because they are usually fed on a regular basis. With humanity's industry, we can insure them against early death. For ourselves, I think we humans want industry of an unusual order as well: the intangibles of life's ultimate meanings, love in the sense of emotional human connection, and achievement of the fullest of self-realization at some point in our lives.

The days continue like moving shadows over and over again with no promise of stopping, save the one I have always suspected as the end and the source of my constant advancement. It will help me stop this insanity. I don't mind the thought of having gotten off my particular perch; it's the getting off, the process of stopping, that kills me. Even so, the actual event, like other tense times, will surely not last long, and I am nervous beforehand about only a few inevitable moments.

My advancing chronological age brings serious thought that life is designed to feel valuable in its ultimate result. I have prepared for days and years and am more than midway in providing for all the goodness and material things that I would ever need. We plan for a point, the apex between two poles, where coming and going meet. We live through this murky point unaware that we have done so, and discovering that we have done it is slightly surprising. We live through this point and fade slowly as we recede from it. Earlier, the future seemed unreal; we did not perceive or understand it; we just prepared for it in a mostly practical way. Now, having arrived at that future unknowingly, I reflect on the journey and determine that I don't have much future left. I now see the line taper to the finishing of the form, the meaning of the whole; the realization that the untold struggles of the past comprise the ingredients and experiments put in place to support the entire structure, which I'm now appreciating for having endured; liking myself finally because the work is nearly complete and not a bad one, and I am able to put these words to paper and to see a shape. It's no longer necessary to apologize about needing the time to think about what's important, about needing to be quiet, retire early, or avoid chit-chat. Being alone does not have to mean being lonely. The more filled, the less lonely.

Should we not recognize the apex of our lifespan? It seems to me that we should recognize the long-awaited arrival of ourselves, when finally we can respect ourselves for having tried

29

and mastered what we, each individual, created, whether in the outer public world or in private where the world is our own configuration to each of us alone. The point of arrival — when much of the past has been played — is the time of conclusion; an almost finished objet d'art may be now be exhibited for our own review. Everyone needs his last ten years to complete for himself the finished work. A short lifespan may not have as intense a summary.

I might vainly say, "I wish to come back as a queen, a king, or a warrior." But "I" could not be one of them because the king, queen, or warrior would not be me! I know exactly what I'm trying to say here, but there's no way to say it since there is no word for "I" that becomes another "I" yet maintains something of the old "I." Why am I an "I" at all? Why don't I feel the personalities of others as much as I feel my "own"? There is no way to describe the incongruous feelings that "I" could be someone else with a different body, brain, and placement in time, but that "I" as now known by me cannot be another person. And what about "coming back" as an animal? What would actually come back in this case? How can I be both what I am and am not? I wonder if death is more important than life since death seems durable. I wonder if "great" beings slowly fade by becoming in the minds of the living just famous names with the "I" of them unimportant.

When I was much younger, I had ideas that for the time seemed a little offbeat, or just "beat," as the prevailing adjective might have described them. Having a body cremated and disposed of like a piece of humus appealed to me as the least infringement on the environment, and this was in a time when cremation was not implemented as much as today. Other times, the oven method has seemed a feat of drama. I've also considered arranging for an inscribed tombstone with a real, although decrepit, body lying snuggly under the ground adjacent. It is a bit of me wanting the taste of immortality with the words, "Here lies. . . ." They would be proof that I existed and could still exist in the minds of those who knew me, or in the case of passersby, I might at least be considered a one-time person. However, I have decided more recently, for the final time, I hope, that I want the young thinker (myself) to prevail for the environment and for tidiness. Regressing to wanting the stone marker is the thinking of the misled. I have rechanneled my thinking on final disposition to my earlier preference along with a host of other conclusions about life and death that I now realize were on track then.

Due to efficiency, I would chose to get rid of the old body by the oven because I can only ascertain the discomfort of seeing or imagining a dead human body that has lain underground for years, or the awkwardness of a technician performing embalming, or arranging for a cement vault for burial. I am not so egotistical that I'd want to tarnish nature with a corpse, vault, monument aboveground, or even an urn. I think a better use for land is to leave it alone for the life it supports. Leaving without burial would save the woods and allow their beauty. No funeral celebration would be my choice. We have our own thoughts to commemorate each passing and our memory to recall the living and don't need a ritual or party or urn to waste time and resources. Yet, in reflective moments, I sometimes I wish my future expired body to be placed casually in a bag under a tree to become part of an ample wooded acreage totally hidden from people and public roads, to provide for living creatures, not to be burned, buried, or autopsied. My guess is that bag and all would disappear sometime during the subsequent two months at the most.

We do not own ourselves finally. After our turn at life, ownership appears to pass to the stagehands backstage and to the appreciative audience or even a non-appreciative one. We are added to the numbers; our illusions as actors are over; we no longer need to blame ourselves for being us; we move to the empty theatre of peace.

Due to my pinch-penny habits and a small inheritance, I now have the means to support myself without having to work for someone else. When I lie on my bed in front of the wood-burning stove, I do not suddenly have to rise up and dress in fashionable clothing to be socially approachable. I can muse and consider life — the meaning of it, the madness of it — a subject I never consider boring. To turn my thoughts to practical action for day-to-day survival does not satisfy my goal of quietude and contemplative living.

Once a year for around a week, there is a snowstorm of the wildest rank in this area, which is not used to seeing more than two snowfalls in a year. Knowing that the bulk of people stay home on these days gives me a fleeting feeling of being part of the rest of mankind, in which I have tried periodically and unsuccessfully in the past to become a congenial, if not entertaining, member. Now, with all persons in this neighborhood temporarily admonished to remain indoors and away from their usual places of employment, club, or charity, I feel like a silent member of kindred in the knowing that we are for a while all together separately, perhaps quietly, and all thinking about things that matter. It is over soon, this storm, and once again a certain awareness of isolation will briefly come to me with the knowledge that my neighbors will have all returned to their groups while I continue chasing the separation.

Some thoughts stream by: my goal to eventually find the sources of runoffs, streams, and rivers; the feeling that cats were designed to survive by appealing to humans by rubbing, purring, and looking soft and adorable; the wherefores for snow falling in a jagged line up a hill, ending in a line of light in an alcove — one of many subjects for a painting seen in odd spaces and cleared areas within a crescendo of land formations; a realization as I grow and grow in maturity that all people have gifts and all are somehow worthwhile in spite of early insults. I wonder if insects operate under something other than raw instinct to survive, if a red cardinal finds it difficult to find a brown cardinal as a mate and companion, at the mystery of the undisclosed places where wild animals sleep, and at the unknown whereabouts of the remains of those that have died naturally. I wonder that someone who had lived many years ago could suddenly spring up again in someone's memory. What is memory? I wonder at the mystery of how possums find each other and at the illusive qualities that make a lovable person as well as a lovable possum.

It doesn't seem appropriate to have elaborate homes in these partially wooded lands. My own land was obviously farmed many years ago. There are rusty implements, an old, rusty haymaker and hay rake, long disused, concealed by advancing trees and weeds. A few acres out front were once plowed with horses for power. Another leftover across the road is a sorghum mill consisting of a rusty tin chimney in an open concrete rectangle, its specific purpose resting under a vague film of time and overgrowth. These mechanical devices remain on the land in remembrance of the little "farmettes" that had allowed trees to mingle with patches used for cultivation in a basic way, far removed from the large and noisy operations of some ugly modern factory farms. The old tools add to the extant charm. Much farther up the road, hundreds of cleared acres that I can see from my car are used for cattle grazing after being logged bare. This has no likeness to the subsistence living of even my grandparents in Missouri in the 1930s, whose tiny pastures were enhanced by the beauty and density of nearby woods. A land without trees is akin to a desert.

I return again and again to my cabin where I am momentarily safe from intruders. What is a cabin without trees? The trees are the parental figures that protect me from the eyes of those who might hurt me. I borrow a bit of the blue of the sky, the white of the snow, the pink of a final apple on the ancient apple tree, the innocence of early-rising daffodils, the determination of the blackberry bushes to spread in every direction, the hardiness of pokeweed and chicory. I combine them in a large mental painting, leaving out the inventions of people: the Statue of Liberty, the streets of Damascus, the facade of the Louvre in Paris. It's a painting with no names necessary for the colors; they ascend into vibrancy or descend into the horizon. Yet it is not entirely abstract nor is it devoid of everything seen. It refers to a first stage, or a last, of Nature, without the pretenses of salespeople or the formulas of academia. It is a portrait of myself without the winking face. I live here before I deal with food, clothing, shelter, and the love of others.

While the painter's brush may wait a while to record feelings in images of color, the written gems of insight may vanish if not harnessed immediately to paper for remembrance. I must learn to carry paper and pencil to catch the thoughts before they fly away. I wish to keep them as mementoes, buds of realization emerging from many moments alone, small trinkets linked to leaves and ground cover. I cannot dismiss the greenery around me because, as the painter knows, feeling must be attached to things. I deal with moments that are often not logical; they could be a bit mystical; and they often have the lure of poetic and even incomprehensible comparisons. I relate my natural environment to conclusions, but I do not preach codes of moral handling or give outright directions to "peopledom." Wonder is my art. For spirituality, I don't need the coldness of text, test, or comings-and-goings of historical human records. I know the exuberance of the child, the laughing, the secrets told, the intense trouble felt when alone, experienced as abandonment. It was everything then and still is a great controller handling the levers behind all my ages. Decidedly later, the little children held within are still my companions and my enemies, and the sunlight still is my hope. I have a longing to paint in words that which would be understandable to those youngsters of years ago as well as today.

Throughout any day, I think and feel scores of snippets, little decorative art forms in colors of words that refer to Nature with a slight twist. These are the pure rewards I wish to record, not the confusing world of the everyday, not the political wrangling or the popularity contests of elite society, not even the basic descriptions of the trees. I want the tiny philosophical crystals left on the path after the preacher's sons and daughters have departed. They are mostly positive emotions, the clear morning of truth through the windows and eyes of Nature: life in its best and purest statements. Should I fail to carry writing equipment, the beautiful thoughts may fade like moonlight on a snowy morning. The notebook and pencil are now nearby, at least; I have yet to attach them to my person. Already, several thoughts have been lost today, but I trust they will come back another morning.

With lovely gems falling into my writing basket, there is no reason to feel lonely or without purpose. Loneliness indicates a void, an incompleteness of one's emotional nature. The wonderful gifts of poetic illumination supercede any human deficit I have and fill my need for ultimate intangible purpose. No people are necessary for companionship, at least for these moments. I need to recognize my field, my woodsy base of operation, and I need to walk toward it. I want to climb with trees, not on them. I shall remain unmolested in places where trees grow unharmed.

After a successful day of thought and contemplation about the apex of my life, I can go to sleep tonight warm and safe and entirely content. I don't need to use sleep as an escape or narcotic to ease unattractive emptiness and rumors about what others have probably determined about life and me. I am creating and polishing my own ideas of what I am about. I enjoy success in a refund never calculated by any accountant. What I have found in 2012 is a realistic outlook on life—the land, the cabin, the thoughts, the peace.

CHAPTER 3

Human and Animal Passersby

Humans

I continue to consider what could cause a privileged human being to seek solitude in a wooded environment. Perhaps I have no talent for friendly gibberish or noises blurred severally together or one at a time respectfully. But especially, more than one other voice puts me on the defensive to get in my own word. Do I need to surround myself with bodies to attain satisfaction in life? I could sit in a group for hours socializing, while debating whether or not to plan for the annual holiday party or raise money for charity. Are the party and the charity really necessary? What environmental resources will have to be sacrificed for them? Perhaps I should stay home and relish a consideration for my own charity.

What is it that I seek from people? Recognition for my supposed talents, a smiling face, "love"? To say that I seek love is much too vague. I could seek love from a possum that, with its irresistible pointed snout and whiskers, seems to say thank you for the leftovers I put in a pan. Do I want constancy from a person always agreeable, verbalizing optimistic paradigms while declaring the world a safe and congruous place? Always smiling, having true love forever? I have sometimes erroneously thought I could seek like mind or acceptance by the groups of humans that I might join: political party, fraternal organization, family social congregation, schools past, favorite charity, ancestral ties, sympathetic perpetrators in religion, if any. Maybe love is related to likeness of ideas about the overall universe, but this does not assure another person would continue holding these ideas or love me back. Even with likeness of thought, I am not guaranteed a feeling of belonging. What if I do not relish joining bands of humans? Should I try hiding in a closet or take another approach? I suppose I could love a flapping fish or a kitten in a tree.

Having been brought up in urban environments with emphasis on school spirit and high office in social clubs, I come now to real relief at no longer having to compare myself to others or having to count the number of my friends who appear physically attractive and happily verbose. My current natural and essential path could have saved me then from worrying about frivolous comparisons, but our way of society pushes youth into such wasteful concerns. I think those who feel positive about integrating into society would not choose to live my way. There is a sort of roadblock in front of them. That same roadblock keeps me from crossing to their side. To some of them, free time does not seem necessary or desirable. They feel they must constantly be moving about and always mingling with others, ever talking if not actively doing. Joining holiday gatherings, reunions, causes, and associations of all sorts to have fun and fill their hole of boredom precludes any question about their fear of embarrassing physical separation. Some extroverts may be empty vessels, unable to surround the environment of the heart with any imagination or feeling of their own. To them, to be quiet is to be confined and deprived and unable to penetrate the hollowness they feel.

The explosion of technology has created a situation where privacy and aloneness are becoming harder to maintain. With the computer, many superficial contacts can be carried on simultaneously, eluding face-to-face and exclusive connection. Fading is the time of genuine relationships when people had only one or two other persons in their lives, a time of familiarity, a time without computers when even the telephone was used with restraint. We can now insult our associates, whom we may not know up close, to an unprecedented extent that might cause lawyers to smile about the rising numbers of confrontations needing defending. We are growing by millions in this country alone, not to mention the world, as we "bump into" our neighbors and business contacts in trivial and time-consuming electronic encounters. We are, or should be, mourning for the few genuine friends lost to mechanical approaches and for the simplicity of nature around our homes and lives once here in the everyday. Left are only faceless shadows and mechanized procedure on the barren pavement of public exchange.

With the almighty home computer and its complex daily functions, we spend hours everyday on email and the internet, messaging, blogging, and typing into boxes. Heaven help us should there be a virus to knock out our work! Checking email every few minutes is common. Being by oneself is to be avoided by the individual who feverishly looks for the immediately recognizable message in the inbox that will briefly relieve his/her dread sense of isolation. Back and forth this person checks email, never being quite fulfilled. This individual sometimes writes a knockout email of his own to send to someone from whom a loving response is desired. Alas, the email sent may impress only the writer, for usually no satisfying and positive response is forthcoming to salve his emotional condition. We do our taxes online; invest our stocks; look up the names of lawyers; form online superficial relationships to cheer us and dissipate us. It is an illusion of togetherness; we are yet lonely.

The norm suggests having a party at every opportunity and saying grace at family meals with family and friends. A preference for being alone to contemplate past celebrations is to be regarded as abnormal; the norm prescribes merriment for present moments, and we should want to plan for shared celebrations constantly. Aloneness can be considered odd, embarrassing, weird, unwanted, unpopular, unnecessary, and despised. You are not needed or wanted, the feeling goes, who chooses to be alone much of the time. My oasis of nature could easily be choked by the invasion of phones, all kinds of hand-held ones, and video cameras, not to mention many other electronic devices of "communication." Cell phones, if left turned on, can reach a person outside and inside in most situations. There are innumerable computer websites and text messaging to tenuously hook us up with other people, minus their faces. To avoid being considered odd, we think we need to be listening, writing, and talking much of the time, at least through an electronic device. Popular thinking is that we constantly need people no matter how trivial the contact. In this case, a "friend" is anyone who will take the time to "talk" to us in any possible way.

To have a relationship that truly solves loneliness requires a substantial willingness to separate from the other "possibles" available to the average person. One can't be successful in numbers of "exclusive" relationships simultaneously from the pool of possibles. I long for that past day when we were lucky to meet one familiar face on the street and value that face. Now, if a face produces vibrations that are displeasing for even a little while, we go to our computers for more social networking to continue searching by the methods available. There are "other fish in the sea," goes the old saying, and it has never applied more than it does to today's situation. It would seem that we still long for another human whom we actually see and know in person from long association. A real friend gained is achieved by working at it. I want to look one person in the face and know he is my friend, but I don't need my budding affinity compromised by the others who clamor at my in-box or my friend's in-box. I want to look out in space and dream about meeting The One, but I don't trust "cyberspace" to help me with that number. I want a particular message in my in-box and it isn't there. How could it be with all the commotion, competition, jealousies, and opportunities for limitless connection?

For a truly compatible relationship, I declare as anathema unlimited talking, sharing every last smidgeon in word form, endless chatter. For a blissful, if it could ever be, friendship, I suggest that each should offer a quiet entity so that not too many byways cross the other's path. Because each of us must ultimately make judgments alone, thoroughly blending minds in consensus is unrealistic. Good relationships involve getting together face-to-face, but the essence of any relationship exists in separate minds, each with private thoughts. We are not lonely for companionship; we are lonely for significance. Personally, I think too much one-on-one talking and in-person togetherness are not preferable to awareness of calm and unspoken philosophical agreement. We search the faces, faces, faces in the streets of our lives, evincing a tendency to be overcome as if by too much wine — or too much email.

Appreciating silence offers the possibility of full awareness, of traversing new corridors outside society's boundaries. Such possibility resides inside each unique brain that finally sees. Over time, such a brain may gain appreciation of nature's trees. My appreciation of nature and aloneness may in part result from earlier frustration, the quietness here offering a more accepting balm and reward for previous discomfort. I find more success in living as I do now than in futile struggles for assimilation in neighborhoods of human congestion. It would probably, however, have made no difference if I had been brought up in a remote environment rather than an urban one, for I sense that my inner nature would either keep me in or direct me to the kind of aura that I find here in the woods.

If one can afford a reasonably comfortable shelter or cabin secluded in nature, especially one that is tiny but adequate to accommodate minimal things for life's comforts, one does not really need to be placed in the arena of arduous friend-searching. Even a single human "love" connection cannot satisfy completely. Nature calls the disenfranchised in love to its door for healing. There is a certain true love in it, though the seasons may turn leaves brown and a detached limb eventually rots. Seasons do not display smiling faces but they don't hate me as they pass.

I am unconditionally succored by their peaceful memory. They were not critical of me while they lived, and they still live in part, encouraging me to do my best work.

A few times, I have found bullet casings and tin cans pierced by buckshot within a few feet of my door. I like to tell myself that this evidence of human activity blew in from the road or from miles away. I have never noticed anyone lurking about. The only incident was when, one dark night, there was a tiny knock on the door. This was immediately alarming because whoever was knocking would have had to pass over a five-foot-tall, locked gate or the barbed wire fence to walk approximately four hundred feet to my door. I had heard no footsteps, just the tiny, almost sinister, knock. I forced myself to answer from inside but finally opened the door to discover a man requesting a jug of water for his car, which he said was overheated back on the road. I quickly supplied the water in a jug, and he left. This event produced no ill effects, but I'd just as soon have no more incidents of surprise tapping occur in the dark. And there haven't been.

✻   ✻   ✻

It must be much more difficult being president of the United States today than it was two hundred years ago when electricity and the media were absent or performing minimally. The presidents of long ago surely had privacy in their stately rural mansions, if not the White House, in rooms not equipped with electronic surveillance. Nor did they endure constant demands for interviews and speeches to appease the public, to be televised, journalized, Facebooked, and insulted daily. Without peace and quiet, it is no wonder that some of our public leaders are not able to make effective hard decisions or carry out campaign promises. Due to the day-to-day subjection of their statements to a public drawn to spectacles, today's too-abundant population is amused by relentless electronic vigilante upbraiding the president and leaders, without fear and without manners. There are too many people, too much government, too much wrangling, too many things, and too much invasive technology. The president is denied availability to the woods along with most of us. Land is surveyed, owned, locked within boundaries, and gagged.

The very social, boisterous types; today's leaders in politics; business executives; and actors would probably not seek the woods. They may prefer land closer to the hub where all properties touch, usually a city, a place where other people are readily accessible on a regular basis. How many persons come alone to deliberately choose a tract of wooded property on which to reside for a pleasant and esthetic experience, pleasing to the eye as well as to the emotions? Around where I live, the majority of locals have been here most of their lives and inherited their land automatically, not questioning the process and not having any reason for leaving. They stay with their families, always assuming they would continue to work the land and eke out a living. Beauty, esthetics, and poetry to be found in the pristine forests do not necessarily enter into consideration.

Getting on with life. Could this mean getting on with family connections: mothers, fathers, spouses, sisters, brothers, sons, daughters, grandparents, aunts, uncles, nieces and nephews, cousins of every description, and grandchildren? I sometimes consider that if I were "blood kin" to the residents here I could "fit in" with people as family while secretly enjoying the qualities of this long-sought place at the same time!, I may try convincing myself: bring me family; oh, how I want to belong! I want to be part of the love and frivolity I interpret in dinner together, marriages, burials, club participation, birthdays, a greeting in every room. Conversely, as a beloved family member, I'd be afraid that the seeing of the land, truly seeing it, would not come. I must be alone, in a sense lonely, to be able to live my exquisite days here. A party atmosphere, even mundane considerations of family activities, would not do. The conversations would converge in practicality and gossip. Chatter would replace meditation; togetherness would imply noise; and special celebrations would produce imprisonment, not peace to see and consider for oneself. In secret, I confess that I'd like nine parts aloneness to one part togetherness, but I'd prefer the togetherness to not take place near Woodscape, or else I might remember it as a place for picnics rather than for probing life's meaning and purposes from the wild. I know myself best in the company of my natural relative, the forest, with whom I'm well acquainted.

Were I to live in close association with others for many hours a day, I surely would regard the privacy of a cabin in the woods to be as remote as a star in Orion, a prize difficult to obtain. It will be an even greater challenge to find woods in the future, always the future that largely does not arrive. I presume the average family, the "happy family," is one of appearances. Never should anyone allow the lucky family to appear slovenly, overly tired and wanting to sleep more than usual, or preoccupied with individual activities and thoughts. Talking with one another— endless vocalizing—is what is expected. The family group must always go places as a unit, admitting only safe allegiances that would not challenge the original bonding. Separations of family members must take place only because of duty to provide economic support or aggressive military engagement. We should not want to leave the family unit for extended breaks of significant philosophical purpose, such as serious fine art or meaningful written expression. A loving family group appears unrelated to, and exclusive of, exploring the beautiful and ultimate thoughts of individual existence. I aim to strive for what I think is really important in life, even if I have to abandon other traditions. It is nice to know I descended from certain stock, and. a quiet animal or two as pets would not seem to conflict with life in nature.

At times, being more vulnerable than I care to admit, there can be moments of awareness of holes in the realm of family and romance. A little family merriment would go a long way for me. Should I be so fortunate (or unfortunate) as to be in attendance at a group of family members, my own or others', I'm sure I would be counting the minutes until I could leave and go home. My family tree has supported my whole life. Ultimately, I always support myself against the backdrop of the landscape where I can hear my own voice. Although a little longing can sometimes result in temporary association with persons who are not peaceful in themselves, such association is quickly unprofitable, taking up valuable time, with solitude giving me relief; here is where I reside. One cannot have human companionship and solitude at the same time; one must choose one or the other. One cannot live all lives simultaneously; one must either recede or accede when encountering the group or Nature.

If not family, I suppose there is some value in "getting together with friends," but the concept of "friends" irritates me at times. What is a friend? Is it someone known since childhood who shares memories, such as climbing trees and playing games, and can be called upon to bring back those days? Are they chance encounters in a specialized activity like car repair, during which one may converse about brakes or vinyl replacement? Are they relatives who can be reached with relaxed rules of family etiquette? Are they one-night stands or part-time companions? Could they include those who have very little in common with us but who sometimes live under the same roof? Do we need people this much? Must we gather people like daisies, piling them up in the blue bowl always gaping before us, pulling one to our hand occasionally to study its petals and scent?

I think there is an unspoken concern that we need friends in case of a health scenario—our own. For some, self-security may include joining causes, moving to townhouses, apartments, condominiums, or at least to a neighborhood of bodies who can be called in an emergency. If we should feel faint from age and drop to the floor unable to arise, as many elderly people surely do in the isolation of their chambers, we think we should not be prone long because our "friends," who constantly buzz in and out of our lives, will somehow *be there* at the right moment to help us, pick us up off the floor, and bring normalcy back. Or, if we die, we still need friends immediately to dispose of our dead body, to notify others, to arrange for dispersal of our belongings and assets. We must continue, therefore, to cultivate friends of whatever kind and duration to guarantee that we will not die unnoticed and humiliated, frightening someone who may stumble upon our corpse days, weeks, or months later. To assuage the ultimate horror, we need friends to help us in our decline, to tend to our personal hygiene, and to pay the bills. To insure that someone will help us when our time is near, we should be on the lookout for potential "friends" now, we quietly tell ourselves.

Since my natural propensity leads me away from groups and crowd behavior or even from gatherings consisting of more than one person besides myself, I suspect that I may die alone. This may not be as awful as it sounds. Surely, I think, while I am still largely competent, I can arrange some answers to my concerns, by pre-organizing to a degree, explaining to a selected few, making a business out of it if necessary, in order to receive a helping hand in sickness or death. These persons may be additionally motivated by promise of payment, if I am so fortunate as to have anything left to pay. As I currently have no plans for energetic recruitment of those who could be counted on should I later become incapacitated, I may just have to be satisfied with the upside of not having an ongoing social agenda now for the sake of easy exit later. I think I'd rather be found deceased after three months than devote long intervening years to trivial togetherness and embarrassing niceties for the sake of long-range planning.

✠   ✠   ✠

There is no ultimate escaping that life has to abide by human relationships of every sort, locally as well as outside one's orbit. We place great importance on the number, if not quality, of friends and of practical and cooperative relationships. Others' faces are on our minds constantly, due to the fact drilled into our brains that we are members of humanity. We never really go far from other people, but I pray to myself I need not slovenly copy the example of others who demand the sight of companions day and night. Life in its importance includes relationships with other people, but must also, above all, accommodate a relationship to self. Relationships with others, moreover, seem to contain those more enthusiastic than the rest. The more enthusiastic might have a tendency to slightly overwhelm while more reticent parties move back. An awkward distance comes between them–the enthusiastic are the winners–but the game continues.

Before I came here, I was obliged to support myself by providing a service that someone would want, creating for myself a kind of human connection of necessity for those who would ensure that my employment be contracted for as long as I needed it to exist. I thereby had a kind of social life, although minimal, through tenuous dealings with women and men, and I did not often feel lonely or isolated. I rarely sought additional human interaction besides my various avenues of employment, since I had quite enough occupation to tire me and, to provide the semblance of togetherness, all the people contact I could assimilate. For more intense human interactions, I functioned as a loner-type, preferring to relate to just one other person in each case rather than to a group of three or more, including myself. If the group had threatened to become three, the atmosphere became a groping for control as competition set in, or two would gang up on the third—not a happy situation. In private moments I wished I never had to be a group member, but I certainly would have been surprised at the solitude that I welcome in my life today. Now, rarely, and only under extraordinary conditions, do I actively pursue face time with real human beings with eyes and hair, even though I feel that old-fashioned interaction through seeing others and talking with them is the best route to friendship.

What will get me up in the morning? Endless chit-chat with my fellow humans, the promise of a nice social coordination for the good of the world? I imagine the universe, which I call my world, would be better off by my not doing too much to it or by leaving it alone entirely, allowing just the shadows and the light through the windows to meet the walls. I need to wake up and see colors and hear sounds with my own eyes and ears. I need to hear, see, and think with a bit of breakfast. To do too much is indicative of having nothing to do, I'm convinced. Look what's happened to the world, my world. We make things better by knocking down this or that tree and end up knocking down a forest and building with the killed trees the malls and rows of houses with public funds collected from the rich and poor alike, increasing the garbage dumps by the highways of most cities. I think I'll just saunter a few feet to a dried-up runoff on my property, which I would rather be an all-season creek A natural runoff, wet or dry, is a valid trait of nature. But society's own runoff of noise, cutting, opinions, spraying, enterprise, words, wills, fire, and hideous transformation is what is left if picnic areas are allowed to spoil a once-solitary and isolated vista, unknown except to a few who remember.

Today, the country's population of 312 million does not seem exorbitant in view of other countries having more than a billion, but back in 1962 the U.S. population was only 186 million. I did the math. It seems we continue to feel we should fill up pristine spaces with more bodies, babies, development, and improvements. I would like to prevent this country, before it is too late, from adding more improvements and more of us. If the whole world could get down to 300 million inhabitants, I would rest my concern. Surely, we could have a more beautiful world of space and beauty and opportunity to sit and dream with fewer of us. How hard would it be to limit the "surplus population," as it was called by Ebenezer Scrooge in Charles Dickens' *Christmas Carol*, by a few simple rules of social noninteraction and some worthwhile efforts of science? Perhaps we wouldn't need as much forensic investigation to nail transgressors if we concentrated on ways to downsize the people, not by murder, but by ethical ways that we are smart enough to know about. World population growth needs to rest. The fewer the people, the fewer the times I would bump into my neighbors on the road, and there would be fewer reasons to confront one another and disturb the peace. A paved or unpaved road is the meeting place, and there are too many people coalescing now on both of them.

Early settlers of this country must have multiplied incredibly fast since, only a few hundred years later, we have people situated from shore to shore, leaving less room for wild animals, which are now obliged to become the playthings, entertainers, and victims (including the main course atop dinner plates) of humans. The rising world population may stop with a new ice age or global warming. Or it could come from the fretful sandpaper effect of too many people going to war with each other, rubbing each other until blood glistens—harming, hating, and eventually driving away the enemy for self-defense or even fun. My world stops momentarily at the consideration of such carnage.

Babies, innocently enough, add daily to the burgeoning world population. Babies often seem to behave like innocent domestic animals, especially dogs, which are unaware of the inconvenience that they instill by their natural processes, such as defecating inside a home on carpets or furnishings Babies, diapered constantly in their own fluids, are no more concerned about anything amiss than the untrained house pet. Yet babies are ogled as "so adorable" by parents and others who may be acting in and directing their own show to satisfy society's concept of good nurturing. Some obsessed adults dote on their babies and young children with endless hugs and verbal regard to the extent of nauseating affection. Yet these same persons may treat animals, including pets, with a lack of concern for their welfare, comfort, and dignity. Dogs are sometimes chained with collars so tight that raw spots appear on their necks, causing the animal to whimper and beg for relief. People would not tie a baby outside even in good weather. People who seemingly love their babies and produce large numbers of them can yet be found raising roosters on chains in small pens for cockfighting. How people can be so outwardly affectionate toward babies but abuse our animal brethren is a mystery to me. I personally find myself rather the opposite: not so amicable toward the prospect of babies who, true to the human propensity for making constant noise, demand our whole attention.

We live in hovels or houses surrounded by bald yards, showing everything on the turf, if not in the dwellings themselves. Is there a reason why we can't be neighbors to trees and weeds to preserve the integrity we see in them and ourselves? In the kind of neighborhood I have joined, I see only trees and the dry creek which activates during the rainy season. No garden, lawn, or landscaping necessary. I have all the beauty I want and some I did not expect. Anything in the woods is beautiful, providing it does not include man the hunter, landscaper, or logger cutting down what will end up as planks for the townhouses of human consumption. A cabin without woods is a surcease from hope.

The automobile accelerates to little beauty on the super-highways, the knife-marks of ruin. May I see nature by driving my automobile on the four-lane to find an exit that, for a few moments, will allow me to see off to the sides the leftovers of road construction, the pickings of nature lost, before retreating in my car back along the monster highway to home? The automobile was designed to enter the smoky business centers with their bricks, pipes, people, and filth. I would have better success finding nature by foot or by the secret and natural paths of the mind known only to me. Limit the automobile and the overall population and it may be possible to find the woods responding.

I always want to take a break from people. I need to slither away like a wild animal from their houses, kitchen conveniences, trains, skyscrapers, planes, politics, stores, workplaces, computers, furniture, and much of their preconceived concepts. I need to give a little imagination to and interpretation of myself profiled against real images of nature and its moods. I need to become a wild animal in my own right. I am relieved to hear that if people, through some disaster, disappeared from the earth, plants and trees would finally begin to recuperate after around one thousand years. All traces of cities and human invention would no longer be visible, and vegetation and wildlife would emerge in original and new forms. The prospect of well-deserved victory by plants and animals gives me a bit of comfort.

As usual, there is much talk of the need for a "good education." The question of what constitutes a "good education" is imperative. Education in business, technology, accounting, or how to press oranges for the most palatable juice all seem only to prepare practically and economically for the life that is supposed to come. I hear enough computer lingo, yet it doesn't keep me from feeling at times that I remain uneducated in the silent and salient mysteries of the world—the lingo is a deceiver. Bring me sophisticated mathematical procedures, but while marvelous, they do not seem to answer some of the questions I have. Archaeology is a bit better; astronomy brings me closer to heaven. If I study computer or automotive science, would I be prepared to frolic with philosophers? Bring me their philosophy or ideas on how to interpret the world that I may tailor them as my religion, to better hear promptings from the profound being that is within me. The arts, certain literature, kindness, and open-mindedness are also likely subjects with homework assigned, not as decorations to fill the time, but to help in interpreting the nature (Nature) of myself and my fellow passersby. Please include a language that I may call mine and that, spoken and written by a standard of correctness, will help prove that I am serious about my education. It is true that the monetary rewards of my impractical education would not exactly clothe a corporate executive, but his occupation would not exactly feed my hungry inner-room executive. Since I have some reservoir from my education pursued from a young age in subjects of meaning, I do not read for entertainment. It must be done for depth, but my inspiration from within is at least as great as the elation sought by others outside of themselves. I seek understanding of basic and general conditions, and I do not scan quickly. I think I'll invite philosophy to be my travel companion on some other back-roads around here.

Animals

Last February, I took my car a few miles down Mt. Hersey Road through wooded land owned by Arkansas Game and Fish Commission. After around a mile, I came upon a very unusual-looking animal standing still in the road, probably around five feet from the ground to the top of its head, a large beast. It had a tan body with a rump of lighter tan and the head of a camel and no antlers. At first, I thought it a deer although I couldn't remember a deer as large and immovable. In my ignorance, I couldn't imagine what to call it. Its big ears flapped back and forth as it stared at me in my car, which I parked around ten feet back. The animal exhibited no fear and seemed stuck on the spot. I couldn't help feeling pity for this creature who had probably stopped in its quest for food during this week of hard freeze and misery, for this area is not used to frigid temperatures and blustery snow. Finally, as I moved the car closer by a few feet, it turned its head and galloped down the road for perhaps a quarter mile before turning into the entrance to an old and hidden family cemetery, letting me drive by.

"There, but for the grace of God," as the saying begins, went I. I perceived the animal to be a loner in the midst of a challenging environment. There was no visible food for it, or if visible, it was visible only to itself. How can wild creatures endure such weather, not to mention hunting seasons that leave many wounded or dead? This one looked to me as if it could use a warm shelter and a plate of acorns. Of course, I am anthropomorphizing.

I assumed the creature managed to arrive at full adulthood without any help by humans. Maybe it was tormented by gun blasts. I identify with it, whose species I do not know, trying to save itself from potential enemies in a place that may no longer have the food it needs to survive. Buffeted like this animal am I, sometimes society-worn, shrugging off from birth the constant barrage of insults, intrusions, pursuit, and displacement to finally emerge miraculously with my inner being still alive. I learned later that the animal I saw that day was an elk.

My thoughts continue to return to a lone brown duck paddling in the slow-moving Buffalo River one day in the fall. This day was nothing special; it could have been any day, any duck just swimming or allowing itself to bounce up and down with the tiny waves splashing near shore. No people around. Alone. Can a duck survive without other ducks? Today, I wonder if that duck is still alive. Where are the dead animals that simply die out in the open? I never see a dead deer, duck, or any other wild animal that has expired.

I have raccoons with babies, possums, and one young groundhog now coming daily to my porch door for the two scoops of dry cat food as well as leftovers from cat and human plates. Other animals may come and leave, and I now see a slim grey fox (which I had thought was a coyote) eating out of the pan. He is a pathetic sight compared to the members of a more robust group of foxes that were here fifteen years ago. He is terrified, constantly moving about on the porch looking for threats to his newfound discovery of free food. I feel for the fox, since it would be his right to eat like any live entity. Why should he have to be fearful when doing it? There used to be more foxes, coyotes, and wildcats. Now, at least deer are still plentiful, although I understand they are eaten in great quantity on my neighbors' dinner plates. I have recently been visited by only the third black bear in over twenty years.

People often say wild animals keep warm due to their "thick coats." If I were placed outside in temperatures below forty with the skimpy coats and no sox such as most of them have, I would be one unhappy animal. How can deer, the ones with the white tails which bounce as they run, abundant here in spite of the hunters, spend every day and every night outside all year in every kind of temperature, the coldest especially? Where do deer go? Where do they spend most of their time? Under trees? Do they really like being exposed to all kinds of weather? Surely their scant fur and hides don't give them satisfaction in every instance. If I had just a furry, or maybe fuzzy, exterior like them, I wouldn't last an hour in truly cold weather. Farm animals and dogs and cats appear better able to adapt than I, although I note farm animals and pets often appear to want a shelter preferably with the humans themselves. Animals may have completely different kinds of thermostats, but I have yet to hear a good explanation of how they can stand unsheltered habitats. There may be a simple answer, but I have not done the research. Yet even if I had the "explanation," I would still wonder.

This morning, I cracked some eggshells and attempted to bury them in the ground to add their organic nutrients to the soil. If wild animals attempted to eat these eggshells, they could scratch their mouths. At birth, animals are no doubt next to their mothers who provide warmth and milk. But after that, they're on their own. Is nature kind to have provided so little food for maturing wild animals that they come to depend on the likes of us? On our eggshells or worse? Furthermore, are they missing anything if they do not contemplate the universe and their relationship to it? Do animals ever wonder even slightly about why they are here?

A variety of animals come to their pan on the porch. I have added birdseed to the mix and observed birds getting used to the idea that the seeds are for them. Birds' heads bob up and down, apparently swallowing the tiny specks whole. How many times must they bob to dispel hunger? How long must I entertain nature

53

to declare myself free from rebuff and loneliness? Are occasional armadillos meant to be my part-time companions? Do they really enjoy being out in the cold? Does raw nature provide enough of what wild animals need without any assistance from me? I feel some concern for almost all animals, including domestic ones who are forced outside much of the time or inside all of the time. Once in a while on the road, I see horses pulling carts that are too big a burden with cargo and laughing humans aboard, enjoying the ride. What do horses think under these conditions?

After eating on my porch, the small animals disappear and I never know where they go or which hole they have waiting. Do they eventually die in these holes? We humans live in holes that are crowded, noisy, and messy. We make a big point of not dying in our "holes," and upon our demise, a big hoopla is made to make public the demise. Why the big time waster? Can't we just privately disappear or permanently stay hidden in our holes like the animals, to be quietly noticed by a kind person later? My thoughts go out to the elk and to the lone bobbing duck, and I will remember them without any funerals especially arranged for them. After the last sun goes out or explodes, where will the duck be then? I hope all wild animals can find a little comfort somewhere, since I cannot offer them much of the food they want, nor do I know much about them overall, but what they need, they surely need now. I offer very few of them only a little of what they need.

☆   ☆   ☆

Outside my doorway, there appeared one day a huge snake, a "copperhead," with a colorful skin of tan and reddish spots, lying motionless in a circle with each curl of its body overlapping the one preceding. I have been told that these snakes are dangerous and some say they should be killed. One method I've heard is to chop them in pieces with an ax. I have never been tempted to deliberately kill any animal with the exception of a few biting insects. The copperhead was sleeping in the sun. I just walked away from it and a few hours later I noticed it was gone. Why can't we let living things alone? Why do we have to kill them without giving them a chance? Some people use animals for entertainment before an audience. They suffer to learn and perform tricks for the empty and miserable humans. Far away from here, there are giant captives from the sea jumping in rhythm from their tanks, funny felines playing at tiny pianos, feathered beings "counting" jelly beans. We need to provide worthier occupations for our animal sojourners and loftier amusements for our fellow humans.

Unless an animal, unprovoked by me, is gnawing at the beams of my home, gaining on me every second to have me as a snack or bloody toy, I see no need to interfere with its natural ambition to live, nor do I wish to torment it by stirring it to challenge me for its life. I am not thrilled to eliminate rodents, but sometimes it's desirable to have them depart from my home; I always feel a certain sorrow if I find a rodent died from the ambitious antics of one of my cats. I sometimes intuitively kill an insect when it bites me or wants to lay eggs on my skin. Fleas and ticks are not to my liking, and I have even less feeling for them when they come after my blood. I do feel the need to find another exit out of my home when I discover a spider's web gracefully blocking the entire doorway to the porch. One night I watched a spider run back and forth over its masterpiece, quite alarmed when I opened my door to gaze at the work in progress. When I put a tiny morsel of meat toward the center of the web, the spider ran to the spot to see it and to attempt to take little pieces of it before determining it was too big to manage or not to its preference. I finally removed the morsel with minimal damage to the web. By morning, most of the web had disappeared, and the spider was leaving quite rapidly, not to grace my doorway since.

Around here, hunting and fishing are practically on every man's agenda. Walking in the woods for sight of a beautiful landscape is not the aspect of nature most hunters describe as enjoyable. In travel brochures, "nature" is mostly described as beautiful and lush vistas, with an oblique mention of the "opportunities" for hunting and fishing, the real purpose of the brochure. The woods, mountain air, piquant greenery, and bucolic pastures shown in photos are mere backdrops for sportsmen shown sitting by the edge of a meandering river or splashing stream, lolling away peaceful hours in the sun with poles propped on a rock. When the actual fish is caught with the hook in its mouth, for heaven's sake, bleeding, struggling to stay in its watery home, painfully gasping and wriggling on shore, the lovely account of "fishing" wanes and the discussion diverts exclusively to the beauty of nature. Nothing is said about what actually comes next—beheading, gutting, throwing away blood and gore in some hidden and private niche—acts too shameful and ugly to divulge. The "sport" of fishing, as presented in a brochure, remains by the side of the river, resting its back against a tree in the dreamy path of the sun.

The hunter of larger animals has even more shameful activities to perform after the bullet or arrow finally subdues a four-footed work of art or a high-flying masterpiece. There are more guts to dispose of. There are sometimes severed feet, organs, and heads with gluey eyes. How can anyone perform these after-kill functions? How can anyone, for that matter, work in a slaughterhouse, the job description of which is never presented in detail to the public, even in expositions of dirtiest jobs, meant to entertain? I confess I am not entirely vegetarian, but I doubt I could love the person who killed the creature that became part of my lunch. The bulk of the world's remaining species could use more of our stewardship instead of our usual determination to subdue them. Thousands and thousands of both animal and plant species have vanished from the planet due to our advancement over the millennia. Killing for sport, with gun or bow and arrow, seems a grueling way to accomplish a better life for animals, wild or domesticated, since death is often not instantaneous but terribly bloody and drawn out.

✳   ✳   ✳

When I see a starving animal, I often invite it to share my warm shelter, give it affectionate scratching, or at least something to eat, providing the animal will not tear me to pieces. On rare occasions, I have taken abandoned dogs and cats to an animal shelter which, although hardly ideal in combining animals in cages, is an attempt to offer temporary reprieve from being subjected to a hostile world. The sight of tormented animals upsets me. While neutering seems like an unhappy event, I can't ignore the fact that animals, especially those we adopt as pets, might be assisted in their survival as a result of it. Perhaps for now, it would be better not to add many cats or dogs or babies to a world already bursting with too many people and pets needing homes.

Occasionally there appear strange animals on my property, each usually alone with its own destiny. Although the first forty acres is completely fenced with barbed wire from four to five feet high, during the fifth summer I heard a strange booming sound on my side of the fence in the part nearest the road. It sounded like someone jumping on large sheets of flexible metal, making reverberations that echoed over many hundreds of feet, as from a metallic drum. The sound continued for several days, and I finally decided to chance the thorns and armature of the brush cover that surrounded the old pond dug by the last owner for his pigs, raised for meat. Finally, in the faint distance on the other side of the pond, I could see a "bird" standing around five feet tall at the head, with huge feet and a long neck and body of down and short feathers. I had no idea what this creature was, and for a moment I thought I had entered a Halloween-like world designed to promote a scary mood. I later found out that the bird was an emu, normally an inhabitant of Australia. Someone, I surmised, must have been laughing behind the closed doors of a farmhouse up the road after they had somehow lifted this animal over the fence into the heart of my land when I wasn't home. Or perhaps the emu painfully jumped over the fence, enduring the barbs in its haste to escape enemies. I know emus like water, but the Buffalo River is almost a half mile away through dense growth. I have heard from the postmistress that some people raise emus for meat. Maybe someone was driving with a truckload of emus and one was dislodged, and over the fence it went for unknown reasons. This is just one example of the constant unanswerable questions that pop into everyday life where I live.

For the next few weeks I carried buckets of water and grain, purchased at a nearby feed store, putting them within the emu's sight. I determined that he or she was not dangerous, but I felt it must at least be lonely and hungry. If I were an emu without my kindred, I think I would be quite aware of my isolation. But I am a human without available kindred, and I am not really lamenting my isolation. When presented with a bucket of water, I would see her (I'll call it a "she") lower and raise her neck in a wide arc to access the water in the bucket, much like a chicken, letting a few drops run down her throat after each gulp. I know she ate some of the grain because each day her bucket needed a refill. My handyman neighbor joined in the effort to make her happy by rewiring part of the barbed wire fence from around the old pig barn, a deteriorating shed, now holding cedar logs acquired after an ice storm. Here the emu could stay out of the rain if she so chose. She did not choose to follow the fence to the pig barn, but chose to stay atop a little ridge while I continued to take food and drink to her daily for weeks.

Even though I couldn't see her from Woodscape, I could still hear the booming sound that I presume emus produce, although I never actually saw her open her beak to utter anything. Finally, one day she wasn't on the ridge; she had apparently walked through the brambly lower front of my property. Soon she walked up the dirt driveway to where I was standing with trepidation. I froze. As she passed, she just looked at me at eye level and kept walking as if I didn't exist. A few days later she moved her headquarters back to a little clearing at the fence, west of where I had found her. I continued to provide buckets of food and water, which daily disappeared, but soon the food remained where I put it and I could only hear her booming faintly; I couldn't see her at all.

She was slowly vanishing. For a while I could hear faint booming sounds coming from the woods near the fence to the west. I know she was still on my property because the sound came from within the barbed wire fence. Then, later, nothing. No booming;

no sign of her. Weeks later, I walked through the property to all four corners looking for her or her body, only to find nothing. It appeared at first that she could have survived here with efforts by me to feed her and provide a shelter. She might have gone on for years living as a solitary creature, without her customary habitat of water in which to swim and without interaction with her own kind. Her disappearance may have resulted from threatening and crazed hunting dogs or an occasional fox or bear. She obviously had something in her brain that told her to keep moving, keep walking in circles, keep trying to find that thing most important to her. What had happened to her could not have been delightful, I'm sure. She may have died trying to find what she sought.

✵   ✵   ✵

Why can't we develop more subtle and imaginative thoughts to amuse us rather than filling up time with sports that abuse and misuse the animals that share the planet with us? We look at their faces, which usually appear innocent as they survey our own faces for signs of admiration. A bull's face is probably no less deserving of appreciation than a human's. How could it have any idea that people could cast it into a ring and watch its slow destruction? What magnificent beast, and those not so magnificent, deserves such painful mistreatment? This includes dog and cock fighting. Since I could never witness such a spectacle, I might suggest a few activities to fill the minds of the real "beasts" who enjoy such blood sport. They could find the landscapes that are left to us, clean up the human litter from back-roads, and remove the unsightly stumps left by loggers; they might find themselves in an important new awareness. Similarly, I pity the human mothers who see their sons stalking each other in boxing or other contrived physical confrontation, such as war. Surely there are nobler activities than these in our "advanced" stage of human development.

Some people regard raccoons, possums, and sometimes groundhogs (also called woodchucks) as "dirty" animals;

consequently they are often "taken out" viciously by nearby human dwellers. In fact, these animals are cleaners of great talent. Because of them, I have no organic trash. In fact, I have no trash at all with the refuse of paper derivation added to my wood-burning stove for kindling. Anything organic the wild animals do not eat is simply thrown out to the waiting woods for assimilation, while unwanted pieces of metal, glass, and plastic are taken to the recycling center in town, a wonderful community asset. In a city without recycling and wild animals, many items would probably be placed in plastic bags and hauled by city truck to a burial place, spoiling the land there. I gained an interesting bit of knowledge firsthand: I had read that groundhogs are vegetarians only, but they will eat meat and dry food left by the cats. I have seen raccoons and the big groundhog eat out of the pan on the porch at the same time.

In average human society, social getting-together often means endless hours spent in shopping for and preparing the ingredients for recipes in kitchen and at stove. There are days spent mopping, dusting, arranging things, hiding things, gathering one's apparel for the occasion. The actual event may consist of persons bantering back and forth, as they sit stiffly in chairs in a single small room. The conversations go on for hours with few really provocative thoughts brought to light. Were I to join the stuffy group, it would not take me long to seek the comfort of a quiet room alone, with enough heat and food and freedom to read and think. There must be blankets, a bed or couch, perhaps an exuberant fire in winter. I'd have the outside trees for companions and no cars or persons coming up my path and no knocks on the door. A warm cat with soft fur would complete the picture. I may take a nap with the animal. The animal says nothing, its face showing only one expression since it does not smile or frown, and its feeling gathers about the eyes, wide open or reduced to slits, staring at me affectionately. A cat's purring is worth more than gossip. Should I prefer sitting with people who force me to listen to words of hurtful intent about other people, or would I rather communicate with the admiring eyes and sounds of an affectionate animal who accepts any stance I might take with the world? The animal, moreover, does not criticize me for preferring purring, privacy, and pulchritude.

The blessings of being alone for contemplation can be acceptable to human individuals like myself, but being alone is not always more desirable in other species. There is camaraderie among cows, horses, chickens, birds, dogs, and at times even cats. The animal groups with its kind. We intuitively think most animals are "dumb" compared to us, and the smaller they are, the more insipid they may appear. But how does a bee know other bees are like itself? I wonder if it looks at them and studies their colors and designs, determining in its bee mind that they are similar and safe for relating? What about chiggers, the invisible larva of mites that cause itching on human skin? Also germs? Where there's one germ there can be many more of the same kind. Often the lone wayfarer of any animal population ends up lonely, attacked, or dead. One time a piglet, out of breath and collapsed outside my back door, had apparently been pursued by dogs through the woods from a distant pasture. I called a neighbor who had outside pens and feeding facilities for birds and small animals. The neighbor, offering a home for the cute youngster, promised good care. Months later the pig had become a hog. After several sightings of it running on the road, the pig disappeared, and I was told it ended up as many weeks of the neighbor's dinners after the animal was "processed" and frozen in town.

I miss the quiet ones who used to dwell here, especially the old mother groundhog, who was so big and furry and used to eat alongside raccoons. She no longer comes out each spring from her hiding place. My spirits were renewed when I saw her each time, sometimes with several babies, one of which I may be feeding now. Something must have happened. Should I have left out more food? Was her hiding place an adequate home? Do groundhogs have a short lifespan by nature? And if the missing all died, why did I not see any dead bodies? The tarantula that had made a small hole near the porch was there for months. It seemed adapted as it peeked out from the top of its hole, scurrying underground at the sight of anything moving nearby. I wonder how long tarantulas live. Would its life have been extended if I had left more morsels for it near its hole? The group of foxes that were here at first, making scary screeches, and a starving wildcat are departed. As I write this, another black bear is my latest arrival to the open zoo. It has eaten out of the porch tray, consuming all of the smaller animals' food. It lunged at me mockingly as I watched the spectacle for a moment from my screened-in door. In spite of its size, I couldn't help but think how cute bears are with all that black fur and round ears sticking out perpendicularly from their heads. My subsequent discovery was a torn screen on one of the back windows with claw punctures in the remaining part of the screen. I'll have to get the screen fixed; surely, I won't have to get myself fixed as well. The other animals don't have a chance at the food with a bear newcomer around. Maybe the bear will decide it doesn't like what I put out. Maybe the bear will shortly begin hibernation.

✻   ✻   ✻

Eventually I have to leave my comfortable domain for the road. The day is fitful: the temperature is in the teens and the wind is rushing and moving my car as I drive. I approach a farm that has pigs, cows, goats, and a dog. I hope that somehow these animals that, I presume, are being raised for meat, the dog being the exception, are at least tolerably warm, especially since life for them is completely manipulated by a human for his own use. The animals would like to have some satisfaction out of life, I am sure. I hope, as I drive near, that the small barn will be holding most of them out of the cold. Today I am relieved to observe some goats and cows inside the open side of the barn, standing near the metal divider. More often, however, I notice animals standing motionless in their barren field, brown and without grass, in horrible weather, the dog included. What kind of life is this for them? What are they feeling or thinking? I would like to have a cow, goat, or pig as a pet, but I must think selfishly about how invasive this would be to me—not the animal itself, but in the procuring of provisions that the animal needs. Food and shelter would have to be specifically arranged: awesome responsibilities.

After living in and around the house of trees for sixteen years, I had the opportunity to buy an additional 120 acres, the wildest and most remote acreage on Mt. Hersey Road, joining protected state land about one and a half miles down the road from Woodscape. With a modest inheritance, I grabbed up this property cheaply without hesitation. Intermittently, for at least a half mile on both sides of the road, may be found my purchase of wooded hills with creeks, especially a vigorous "wet weather" Davis Creek. A house could not easily be built on such rugged and angular property, although long ago loggers had a bonanza here. I am hopeful that the vandalism I've experienced by someone's removing my "private property" and "no hunting" signs and metal fence posts has ceased. I would like to talk personally with the person, or persons, responsible for the misdeeds to share ideas about our common goals. To any question arising about what I'm going to do with the property, I reply that it's nothing I'm going to do with it. If it's nothing I'm going to do with it, then that's everything to me.

I bought this land to save the sunlight and shadows of the restorative environment of nature before it is taken away. Nothing shall be built here. The only nearby residents live in an old farmhouse and pump their water directly from the all-weather gushing spring near their doorway. I would prefer this esthetic land to an elegant city home any day. It's terrific prosperity to own these rescued hard-won acres, but nothing quite affirms my existence more than the first forty acres I bought in 1990 and the little cabin built to fit my wants and needs and sometimes those of the animals.

The winter is going to end soon, I'm hoping. For several months, I have been indoors inventing my written recipe from natural ingredients, stirring my imagination seasoned with summer memories and spiced by autumn. Spring shall then come, and I trust it will ease the bizarre nature of this inhuman winter. Nights of single-digit temperatures prevail, and snow inhibits and alarms me when it covers ice. But I have shelter and animals, unlike some people, and an expected dawn of warmth to bring buoyant energy. I anticipate new life soon.

BOOK II
Wanderings

In the summer of 1961, when I was twenty-one, I made the effort to discover physical nature — trees, rocks, grass, hills, creeks, pastures, and woodlands. I departed New Jersey's sprawl and headed for the tiny community of Portage, in north central Maine, where I remained from July through early September. There I rented a fisherman's cottage near the lake and found the remoteness I sought.

FAR HILLS, NEW JERSEY
OCTOBER 1962

CHAPTER 1

Heading Out

Thoughts Before Departing for Maine

My ancient and primitive forefathers lived a very different type of existence on the plains and in the forests than my life in urban comfort. Pushed by their sense of survival, they spent their lifetimes providing for hearth and hunting their supper. They struggled and bared their limbs to the test of crude nature. What bravery they had to know! What pain they must have endured! Yet what did it get them, other than the opportunity for blind reproduction? Their brains were numbed by storms of the sky and by infertility of the land. Nature to them was less beautiful than brute, being mostly a force constantly threatening to snatch away their frail lives. I jest when I say I rejoice in the realization that I am evolved from my ancestors and that my "very desirable" occupation in a warm office sitting at a machine typing sales records of other machines secures me in A.D.1962, urban America.

I am almost free from monumental struggle for bodily needs. I am removed from labor on the land for the harvest of crops. I don't even have to coax it with an occasional spade or shovel, confident that each day my food is being gathered by agribusiness. I need not worry about weaving my clothes; I may buy them already sewn and styled. I rarely have to walk, since I ride a bus with a high-powered motor. I do not need to participate in sports, since there is just as much pleasure in watching a few energetic ones on the television screen. I clean my house mechanically; I wash my clothes mechanically; I even sometimes wash my dishes mechanically.

In contrast to my forefathers, I am blessed with a portion of leisure. Leisure, for me, is that time that I am not sitting on my office chair; it affords rest from my so-called challenging job. I read exciting fiction, watch sports contests, or take up the pastime of collecting stamps — tiny pieces of paper made by machines. Sometimes I even tinker with the starter switch of a motor-propelled boat, which sends me gliding through the cool summer breezes. The fact that I am able to tinker with such a switch is the result of the evolution of man's ingenuity for invention. Most of all, I love to sip a hot beverage from my cup made in Lisbon while warming my feet on a radiator in the den. I often find others who wish to play games with boards and pegs. In the morning I awaken for another boring (I admit it) day at the office. One might say that my world is a machine, yet I am reassured that my life is more meaningful than the painful life of one of my ancestors who roamed the deserts and who had no opportunity to search for a job behind a desk.

The affirmation of yesterday is today's error; likewise today holds tomorrow's misconceptions. What voice, what regulation of culture, remains with unyielding perseverance? What stern prejudice, what rigid etiquette, what post, what grand object shall not meet the test of time? What creed, what formula for social admiration, can resist? In town, I meet the ruler, mass-thought, who speaks of motor vehicles, politics, chain stores, government, religion, industry and markets, corporations and businesses.

This is the age of technology and invention. It is a cult of the grand and glorious things. As for knowledge and research into science and history, there are those who are devoted to their laboratories and to their university lectures, who operate for mankind as a whole, for all the individuals. More labor-saving inventions will likely be the main result. I, too, in a sense, am in a laboratory searching for new discoveries. I am told to buy two cars, a playpen for a future baby, and dishes with a floral pattern. In my home I must install a washer, dryer, heater, beater, toaster, squeezer, and an electric can opener. It is assumed that I pay my water, heat, and electric bills. I am told to go into certain stores because they are cheaper and larger than others. I am urged to smile at all people and call them by name. I am advised to talk on the phone to fill the silence, don a special uniform that convention has woven, and retire at an acceptably healthy and decent hour.

All varieties of foods are deemed important. These include pies, oiled salads, frozen creams, pickled condiments, seafood cocktails, mashed and casseroled vegetables, garnished meat platters, delicate appetizers and teasers, cakes, aged cheeses, and drinks to twist and take the mind. Yet what value is the attractiveness of the food, the smoothness of the beaten mixtures, or the delicacy of the taste? For what is the dough for cookies, or ingredients for a meat sauce? Why is there a day taken to prepare a feast that leaves no time for nature? What is there about the taste of a dark liquor that stands in the stead of unaffected inspiration?

You complain, mass-thought, if I wait too long to cut my hair. The shirt I wore yesterday I wear today and you are upset. I embrace in the street to honor a friendship and you look out your windows in disgust. I must swallow a medicine for every one of my disconcerting aches, consider rigid and standard training of offspring that may result from my normalcy, and you instruct on correct procedure to have them be born. My home must be tidy and with no dust to spite my shelf, even in the basement. I must bathe everyday, must use special soap in my hair and astringent on my cheeks. If I do not file my fingernails, I deserve punishment by you.

Mass-thought, you continue with your loud advice. You say that I must obtain insurance to reinforce my old age; that I ought to buy stocks and bonds; that I must fill out applications, sign agreements, and pay for licenses. You allow me to go onto my well-manicured lawn to look at the trees after you have acquired my admission fee of mowing and trimming. I am told to give to chest drives, to health funds, to little children's camps, and to old ladies' rest homes. If I do not join organizations or call on neighbors, I am odd, lazy, unsociable, and unpopular. I must not forget to be proud of my flag, my nation, my democracy, my freedom, my religion.

My home must go out to other homes, other nations, you continue. You profess to ignore no race or economic status, while secretly urging me to segregate and exclude. While you exhort me to remember the nations, to respect their doctrines and their moralities, you would have me patronize only one creed, which claims to contain the significance for my own country if not the universe. Especially, mass-thought, you prescribe moderation and love as the ideal while you secretly advocate stealing grand objects and wealth in dishonesty or war.

This is the Age of Conformity. You say I live in the Age of the Great and the Grand? Shall not your dwellings, clothing, and doctrine of social acceptance all fall to the ages of tomorrow? How grand and glorious are these—these objects of impermanence? I had always imagined Truth to be something permanent, something that remains after the winds of the earth have calmed. What is there in this culture that you would have me follow because of such resiliency?

How can I waste this evening?
In a door? In a face?
In some disgrace?
In law? In oath
To a great gift: growth?
This is my time;
This is my personal shame.

Thoughts After Arriving in Maine
July 6

Yesterday, I flew in a small aircraft from Newark to Presque Isle, Maine, and arrived in Portage, where I found my lodging.

Portage consists of a general store, post office, and unpretentious homes near the town lake. Illumination was near. It was a day filled with trees. From the tiny community I found a beaten earthen road, hardly used. On one side, five hills rolled and roiled. On them grew little black trees with green apples. The trees and grass played mysteriously with the wind soaring through narrow valleys. The day was a spell; it was singularly dark; grey clouds hung over the horizon like boulders. As if driven by a fever, I kept walking out into the bleak atmosphere, arriving at the summit of a hill. It seemed as if I stood on the precipice of the world.

This is a place where five hills bind
And tree forms borrow the wind;
This is the spot on which I stand
With feet broad on the ground.

Wind seemed to rush through me the way it always did. I felt almost carried away by it and by the peculiar, interminable land and pessimistic fog. Perhaps it was the dismal weight of the clouds that leaned over me. Perhaps it was the bouncing of the green crabapples as they caught the attitude of the commanding wind. Perhaps it was the ground that surrounded me and then swept away to the horizon. Maybe it was the wind itself as it prepared the storm in the clouds. How likely are man's inventions and earthly things to be torn apart on the precipice where five hills meet! I returned to town just as the storm broke.

When the paths of men and cultures terminate in permanent darkness and decay, there still remains the site upon which they once stood. I believe that trees and plants still remain, and mountains still touch the feathery noses of the clouds. I believe crawling and slimy possibilities continue feeding under the tonnage of ocean fathoms. Still shining is that fantastic bulb, the sun, and the moon still follows the earth yet clinging to its orbit. I believe there still operate dynamic and weighty processes that form mountains, crush rocks, move continents, and cause eruption of volcanoes. I hope that silent trees overhead still preside over magic shadows in a river's flow.

And when it is all concluded,
Behold it is as before it arose:
From swarms and troupes
And crowds and groups
Come woods and streams
And hills and dreams.

Why should I come to the hills, the bending trees, the storm, the precipice? Why should I listen to the wind whisper in and out of the valleys? By what means may I trust its companions, the lengthening clouds? Why should I bond with swaying branches on this vast and interminable land?

It is the ground in which I believe. It is the ground that was the floor of ancient Greece, and it is the ground that is the platform for all societies, including complex society. Ground, I have faith in you. I recognize you as the most unchanging and unyielding entity throughout the echoes of my consideration. You are the firmament of all nations, all races, all sects, all time.

I salute the land, the harbor of my soul,
My origin, my village, and my goal.
I left the city like a blast behind;
It was not pretty and my soul was blind.

July 8

There were many days, many adventures ahead. A new day. Just outside Portage I walked in a field of tall waving grass into the horizon. My feet became mud-ridden, sinking into the moist earth. My legs were scratched by unfriendly and sharply tipped weeds. The going was slow, but looking back occasionally, I could see a lengthening trail impressed in the grass. As I approached a ridge, my feet began to carry me more rapidly. I was encouraged; I was rising to the earth's crest. When I arrived at the highest point, I was unprepared for the sight of the field descending on the other side of the ridge and ending in a woodsy clump. I stood on the summit, motionless. The uncomfortable feeling of my feet and legs was not in my mind.

Again, I saw the ground. The grass was thin on the ridge, and small areas of the rough soil could be seen through blades waving as individuals. Pebbles distinguished themselves with light in a pool of water near a rocky opening. Looking into the pool, I saw my hair with branches of trees and the grass and clouds, the hypnotized victims of the wind. All — the branches, the grass, the clouds, and the hair — were bending with a flowing movement in one direction. Everything going in one direction. Looking into the pool again, I saw my eyes.

Vital for me is actual experience — the seeing, hearing, and breathing in the making of images containing feelings, opinions, truths. There is some value in considering the experience of others recorded in books. There is some insight to be found in the content of one's own dreams. But there is no image that compares to that which is an impression of a place where a person's own body has been and seen. Imaginary images that rise up in the mind are apt to fade like the night yielding to the dawn. More substantial are the remembered images once suffered by the senses, enabling a man to be truly alive, like me this summer in the environment of nature.

I use my own mind, interpretations, senses and feelings at the scene of nature. I think through experience. What is important is the moment I traverse the ridge of the field, that moment of special awareness, of its fleeting. In that moment, I feel life in its significance, the moving underlay of my practical efforts. Shall I mind whether someone else looking up beside me feels in the stars a truth that appears to be different than mine? Shall I be despondent if, in the face of the same environment, we feel differently? No. It is enough that individual feelings are translated from a natural foundation.

I walk the fields; I throw stones in a creek; am I wasting my time? Am I merely walking, throwing stones? At last my time is not cluttered with tasks to accomplish, places to go, and fiction to read. I am free to devote my attentions to what supposedly I had been devoting my attentions before: Life. I have reached the point wherein I have nothing to do—I have reached it with effort—but wherein I have everything to do. This everything is woven in my mind while I am called idler, loafer, time-waster. I have nothing to do; I have only Life to seek. I must admit that the environment of nature this summer is basic for the greatest rushing and swirling that I could achieve. Only now can I partake of the wonderful heartbeat that I had faintly, but constantly, recognized beneath the confusion of activities that had engulfed me before coming here.

Nature demands attention, and while walking through a wood, one must push away lingering thoughts of the affairs of men. The lessons of nature will not be maintained without effort. I need my mind interpreting, expressing, and yielding my feelings in actual experience. But experience in nature that misses the full concentration of an individual is not in vain. He may walk through the landscapes again; insight can be "brought back" and developed after a day or years. Complex society is so stuffed with expected and "normal" things to do that it almost requires an exceptional recluse to clear the debris from his mind. Retained pictures of Nature can rescue him. Remembrance of Nature's images will define me now and later.

I grow tired of walls; I desire to go where the trees are, to experience nature's landscapes, to be unified with the rushing of the senses. I see the stars, feel the skies, penetrate the fields. I wade on the shores; I am blown by windy spots; I canvas for wild flowers but leave them to grow. I take in my hands the leaves of the environment, the roots, and the mossy blades. I let their reality skim my forehead, taunting my face. By touching parts that had been overlooked by society, I am trusting myself, defending myself, inspiring myself, beautifying myself, getting acquainted with myself, being kind to self and to my planet. I enter an environment, the purest being Nature, in the times when I have nothing to do but weave the best story of my life and its realization.

I lay flat on my back in a wheat field, letting the wind rustle the grass beside me, my eyes tugging the clouds above me. When the tall grass bent overhead, I felt like an angel in a summer paradise. The turquoise sky with the vibrant yellow of the waving earth was a cleaner world, a more valid world than the unreal world of human convention and invention. In times like these, the codes of behavior that echoed from the complex world were feeble; there was nothing left except myself and the surrounding countryside. There was little to do except see with my eyes the veins and the green of a single leaf and to consider the reason for its existence.

The summer seems to be the best time to explore places where there are few roads, few hampering conventions. In summer a man is free to toss about his arms; in winter he keeps his arms wrapped around his shivering frame. In summer a man may gaze at many fields; in winter a man is confined to the space by the hearth. Summer is a time to jump about and race on the hills; winter is a time to reflect upon that jumping and racing.

July 15

I could have gone to a fabulous city. I could have gone to foreign shores. All sorts of architectural and cultural establishments called me from their gateways. They called for me to taste their foods, to enter their market places, to feel the thrills of new customs, to witness assorted religions and museums of humanity. I didn't hear them. I came here, to these woods in Maine not yet too altered by civilization.

From a stroll on the paved road, I turned into the fringe of woods where predominating were white birch trees from which old bark stood out, dried, leaving patches of reddish-white skin underneath. An earlier rain had made a few of them shine with glistening smooth surfaces. There was also the pungent smell of pine.

I was guessing the name of the pine. I came here not knowing the names of the growing things. I can hardly tell a weed from a flower, bush, pine, or cedar, and I have little knowledge of the names of many animals that may inhabit the area. In spite of not knowing the names of the flora and fauna, I feel attuned to nature's forms. I do not need to look at trees in terms of nomenclature to sense my relationship with them, significant beyond words.

My attention turned to the little trees emerging through the abundant ground cover. They rooted close to their parents the way the children of mankind do. Their thin stems and bright green leaves did not yet know what it is to struggle through storms, did not know what it is to be tested in physical nature. Probably most of them would die for lack of sunshine; there were too many saplings to reach the height of mature trees. One youthful tree was older than the others, but it was not an adult. Its sunlit leaves stood out on a background of subdued shapes. It was a pleasing arrangement of darks and lights in the depiction of departure from immaturity.

I discovered that this wood was invaded by small deserted cabins, probably built by long-absent lumbermen or hunters. Crumpled newspaper and food wrappers lay nearby. As I wanted to be released from the reminders of humanity, I kept moving swiftly. Approaching a railroad track on a bluff, I hesitated; the track also represented men and their concepts, and I longed to see something else for a change. I turned off the bluff for another part of the woods. The forest floor was covered with wet leaves of a summer ago, dead petals of aged and younger growth, reminding me that all things separate inevitably and fall to the ground as broken elements. In no ways but by parting does death occur, making way for new life to emerge in vague probability. Although some of the dead leaves had evaded being broken during the rough winter, in time the ground would absorb them. One moved and cracked; a worm from the ground below suddenly came to the surface.

I still did not feel alone. In the distance could be heard the noises of distant humanity. Perhaps I must travel great lengths into nature before I can break ties with the human world. Nevertheless, I saw what I could of the woods. After a long period of climbing, I reached the top of a hill where the trees, straight and tall, made verticals frantically racing before my eyes as they sped away from me at lower levels. Moss provided a soft mattress under my feet while, through the leafy ceiling, dots of sunlight fluttered. Although I could still hear human reverberations, they did not detract from this world apart.

Suddenly a bird interrupted with a strange chant. The notes, issued at intervals, bounced on each tree, and I surmised that together they would be a chord in the stillness. I felt like an intruder in the paradise of a solitary bird. Suddenly the bird, which I never saw, stopped his concert. I felt peculiarly alone.

As I walked, the moss on the ground thickened. Broken and rotting trunks, their struggle for existence concluded, soaked in the green mat with white and charred sticks left from rains and storms. I leaned against a tree but startled when it collapsed behind me. The bramble was thick. I became aware that I had come into a place that I didn't know how to leave. I looked for paths made by men, but the obtrusive underbrush made it obvious that there had been no clear trails in this place for a long time. What appeared as paper and pieces of cloth were only pieces of white skins shed by the birch trees. My steps hastened. My hands tore at the limbs obstructing me. I ran. I stepped in a mud hole. I listened for the sounds of men, concepts, and ideas. I heard something like them in the distance, but now far in the distance.

Moments later I came out on a narrow paved road. Where had I been? In which country? On whose property? What does it matter? I could have been in any time, in any state, country, or property. These are only words like the names of the trees.

July 16

The gardens I leave to the city. The gardens I leave for filling voids. But there is no void here. There is the complete and rounded personality of nature. No man need come and cultivate that from which nothing has been taken away. A garden would certainly be lacking in comparison. After explaining to some of the staring members of the village that I wasn't "lost," I quickly dashed from the dirt road onto a path in the woods, showing no abandoned cabins or railroad track. After yesterday's warning I initially didn't object to using a path, especially since the dry leaves on it were unstirred and offered guidance. At least there were no revealing traces of newspaper or food wrappers.

The wood was dark and alive. Trees growing very close together admitted little light, creating seclusion enhanced by the absence of sounds of human commerce. Small droplets of dew on leaves were luminous and tempting. When a little thirst developed I managed to roll some of the droplets onto my tongue from the surface of a broad palmate leaf. The floor of the forest sported violets in patches both in mud and dry ground. This was the first time I'd seen violets growing in other than gardens, backyards, and sidewalk cracks. While comparing a white violet with a purple one I startled at a peculiar stirring, but it was only the rustling of treetops encouraging the scurrying of birds or chipmunks. The same daring melody of the solitary bird of yesterday presented itself and soon blended with the growing chorus of many birds. The whole forest sang.

I followed the path until it suddenly ascended to an embankment, a huge grassy arena surrounded on all sides by woods, probably where farm animals once grazed. I waded through the grass to the other side of the arena and stood on an old log. In the grass could be seen the path which I had made from the dark cavern opposite. My eyes wandered to the hills. The nearer hills could be seen as speckled dark and light greens. Tall cedars stood as black forms against distant hazy hills stretching across the horizon. All hills probably look blue at a distance, I thought. My eyes caught a dazzling ray of midday sun. While I know that I am a live thing, heading ever onward from birth, I am able to see in nature a portrait of myself. I compare the morning sunrise to the bursting, growing, dependent days of my childhood; the noon sun to the exaltation of my maturity; while the declining afternoon and night lead me to the inevitable darkness that, after all, is the only permanent reality in the infinity of space from my earthbound perspective. Here in this brightly lit noontime was Life's present portrait, and no images of men and concepts invaded the harmony.

The simplicity of a fluttering leaf reminded me that the innovations and traditions in society had shown me complication and confusion. This leaf was the concise style of a basic environment. After the basic needs of the body for food and shelter are satisfied, there is for man the simplicity of nature. Perhaps the blank mind, or dreamy rest, is simpler than even this fluttering leaf. Perhaps Life is closer to a state of sleep than I had imagined. Perhaps when I see and feel the peace and bliss of nature's woods, hills, and fields, I am looking at symbols of uninterrupted rest.

I continued into the next woods where the sunlight occasionally glimpsed. Between the forks of the limbs of a large mature tree could be seen a cluster of young trees in the distance, illuminated by the daylight, which emphasized their light young leaves. Then appeared a tree around which no other trees grew. I found one side of the tree was alive and green, but only stark grey limbs with pointing spears flew from the other side. There did not seem to be any disease affecting that side, nor was the tree burned.

The woods ended in a place where devastation had taken place—where men and machines had torn roots from the land, had made trees lean over and die, had made hurt and suffering for them. I tried to overlook the white tree skeletons scattered like unburied bodies on this assaulted land while my heart went out to the huge root networks below and aboveground, which had operated the processes of life and were now the victims of men. What would it take for men to be more quiescent and accepting like the living trees?

Dare someone to recklessly chop down a place of beauty like this one, and I shall wonder about his willingness to cause wasteful destruction. I would ask him to please stop trying to conquer the wilderness, stop looking upon nature as an obstacle but as the sacred origin, village, and goal to seek. Near this devastation was a pond created from additional disturbance by machines. Even though the pond was muddy, it was still supporting life; I could see every twist of every plant growing on its bottom. A few remaining trees weaved arcs over cloudy water in a narrow inlet. On the surface of the water, insects were playing tag. What a way to spend the day—hopping about on the water, playfully bumping into one another! However, soon I sensed that this "playing" was not really fun but something inherent in the character of the insects, something necessary for their survival.

Later I found a cozy thicket surrounded by sturdy cedars leading to the sky where clouds were moving away from red explosions before the sunset. I felt elated as if I were almost able to garner a secret usually concealed by a fluffy shield. Thus, by looking all around — upwards, frontwards, sidewards, backwards — to nature and studying it with eyes wide open for close observation, I commanded the sides of my personality that had been hidden.

A pair of birds became angry. Their violent fussing and furious flying prompted me to find the dirt road leading to the main pavement. After walking a while on the steaming surface, I concluded that not only woods but paved roads can lose a man in their branches. With a tired decision, I reversed my direction. It was not long before I observed an expanse of land to the side that I had hardly seen when I passed it earlier. Virgin timber stretched for miles and speckled hills faded and faded until they became a haze. Layers of clouds picked up where the hills ceased.

July 26

I wanted to turn off the paved road after getting a feeling of being wondered about by the populace of the community. Little children giggled and questioned me about the contents of my knapsack, and both women and men stared at me from their yards. One man asked who I was and, of course, if I were "lost." All of them gave me an uncomfortable feeling, but I was determined to continue my adventure in spite of them. I am not afraid of refutation. I am not a lawbreaker and cannot be judged except by me. If my interpretation of the world is bad, it is bad only to myself. Similarly, if it is good, it is my good. If others do not give me the right to judge their ideas of the world, neither have they the right to judge mine! My heart is my own, and I assume no one will step on me.

My soul longs for the discovery of itself. I would gladly suffer a few hours for the minutes that reveal myself to me. I would gladly leave my clan, my populated habitat, to walk with myself alone. I have always seen the world in terms of interpretations dictated to me. But now I long to have that Interpretation which is different from the others, which is my very own idea of the world.

The main road turned quickly out of the populated area to the railroad track cutting through dense woods. Soon I was alone. It was a grey windy day, and down the track came potent sunlight like a shining beacon. Perhaps around the turn was a lake or mountain. Or perhaps there would be a view of valleys below the level of the track, or of hazy blue hills on the horizon. My attention soon sidestepped to the crows. A big crow on a cedar was loudly cawing, warning his companion of the danger I represented. His yellow beak snapped open and shut. His mate, concealed in a distant tree, was patient in listening and waited her turn to utter, but the first crow consistently and harshly interrupted her attempts. Their interaction was a unique language of intensity.

Continuing on, I was overtaken by another loud and muscular sound. Laughing like a hyena, it sounded like the din of some threatening carnivore. When the sound stopped. I stood still. I took a step. I tiptoed on the track. Suddenly a boisterous squawking bolted my nerves. I retreated running, but turned around when the noise stopped again. I walked briskly towards it, seeing nothing and trying not to pay attention to my fearful anticipation of the creature. Abruptly a huge black form flapping its wings flew from a vine by the track into the woodsy interior. Just another crow.

A few tadpoles or undeveloped frogs were traveling with the runoff in the ditch at the side of the track. It was a grey windy day, and when the wind stirred, unseen bullfrogs began to exercise their throats, making booming sounds. As a child I had passed many hours watching tadpoles, and I felt that same engrossment as I surveyed their antics. Individually they varied as to size, length of periods for resting and swimming, and force of their tiny tails. In general they stopped, moved, then stopped again. It was obvious they did not want to move with the current; they sought the protection of the quieter water around rocks. Taking a stick I scooped out an area for a little pool to form undisturbed by the current. Not many tadpoles moved all the way into it; to help them out, I touched their tails with my stick to guide them. Some of the tadpoles were swept over the top of the pool by the pull on the other side. They seemed to have no particular destination or goal; in the pool they kept flashing their tails back and forth through the same water. Just for a moment they seemed like those in the world of men who flash back and forth in the same routine.

I left the primitive life of man to join the civilization of the animals. My thoughts of man had once regarded man as so important for his economic accomplishments that I hadn't really noticed the animals. Perhaps this was because animals don't make as much noise. Animals don't cut the trees down (except for beavers). Animals don't build great buildings or underground subways. They don't fill up silence with words, custom, and politics. They don't feel nature as a void. In this sense, animals are more sensible and naturally enlightened. I have seen few animals on this trip, but I have an idea how they think.

Starting back, I observed that the pine trees to one side of the track were taller than some of the storied buildings in complex society and exceeded the diameter of my torso. Their long and heavy branches waved contentedly in the wind. Tiptoeing into the woods, I saw the vigor of giant trees sustained, but everywhere else the wreckage was enormous. A black underbrush opposed further entry with decayed branches and trunks. Broken vines streamed about, forming discs in the air. Even the trunks of the standing rulers were beaten and scarred while knifelike gashes into the heart of a few exposed vital fluids. It was as if the woods had engaged in a gigantic conflict until the victors emerged as the tallest and strongest trees in the forest. This was a swamp kill; it could have just as easily been a saw kill by man. Here I was desolate like this picture of the woods. Yet the woods were desolate like me.

Decaying limbs half emerging from the earth at first appeared to be safe places on which to step, but when my foot sank into the mud, I learned that the limbs were floating in green slime. Thus I cannot enter some woods even though at first sight I may think I can. It is due to the impossibility of acquainting myself with all features of nature that my interpretation should be open to many evolving shapes. I would prefer to remain vibrant and strong in nature even if some acres fall away and separate from me. I feel better just thinking about evolving.

Nature is my supplier. I find the forms there and shape them into interpretations intimate with me, with my secrets, accepted because I have already accepted nature. My interpretations are myself—my soul. From all directions, the world of concepts, ideas, and material industry has markers and signs to lead me from my interpretations. I prefer the ways of the woods more than the consideration of the railroad. How far we can come away from ourselves.

August 5

I came here a month ago bringing little more than a few articles, namely, sturdy clothing. I brought some pencils, notebook, and drawing paper too. If I needed further entertainment than the woods, I would suspect myself of being vacant—perfunctory—and of not being as abundant and as varied as the trees of nature. I did not bring any books on natural science or on philosophies and religions of other men. I have read some of them, and none of them taught me the feelings I should have or the interpretations that are right for me. All they did was encourage me to do my own research. I did not even bring a dictionary. (That came later.) For now, I am confident that the elementary words I use are applicable to my soul. My soul, like sincerity, is not too complicated to comprehend.

After receiving the usual stares, I turned off the paved road into a rolling field leading to a crest. I am safe so long as I don't linger near the merchants on the road. By choosing the undisturbed view, I am free to own the world. Upon reaching the crest, I could see the verdure stretching to define the hollow bowls of valleys in the pasture below; heavy sunlight blurred distant forms. Treetops of cedars managed to cast long shadows. How likely in the years to come will people beg for room, plead to partake in the spread of these valleys? Will they also cut the roots of the remaining forests? How much longer will natural forms remain abounding?

Placing my knapsack as a pillow, I lay in the green cover, limbs casually flung at my sides. Behind me I could hear bees invading a bush of pink blossoms. In front of me I could see the grass rising above the level of my nose. Peering out one eye I saw the rounded tip of my nose, the pointed leaves of the grass, the turquoise sky intermingling with the grass, the clouds, and half-encouraging sun. The curve of my nose belonged there as much as the grass and peeping sun.

Today was a grand and sunny summer's day. As I lay on the ground, I'd think pervasively of things, the remnants of last summer and summers before that. I found myself striving to hang onto more youthful stages—the vibrant laughing and running child who thoughtlessly played in fields like this. Although I cannot be that child again, at least I can reach for her and attempt my own rejuvenation by coming to summer places.

> *I went to the woods to find the words once*
> *Knifed within a tree,*
> *I went to the woods to find the thoughts of*
> *Years ago by me.*
> *I went to the woods, the greenish den, which*
> *Sped my feet to jump,*
> *I went to the woods and tripped upon a*
> *Wicked sickened stump.*
> *I went to the woods and cried and mourned for*
> *Beautiful words cut down,*
> *So I wrote them again with the point of my pen*
> *On the stump and stumbled on.*

I delight in the passage of the days. I grow with the natural forms. Nothing should keep me bound to a limited showing of nature as nothing should keep me bound to the limited exertions of complex society. If I am confined to one area, to one aspect of nature, I shall have a limited point of view. I come to the simplicity of an open and sky-filled field from the simplicity of shady and wooded areas. In new discoveries am I daily re-created.

With the sun completely hidden, the clouds became balls of smoke and were getting smaller as they stretched to the horizon. I had never really looked at clouds before, I concluded, for they were not truly white at all. They had different intensities of grey throughout. I fixed my eyes on two particular clouds. One was big and bulbous except for one sharp indentation. The other was tiny and shaped like an arrowhead. The point of the tiny cloud was sailing straight for the indentation of the large cloud. The big lethargic cloud and the little agile cloud were partners in dissimilarity, and they looked like they knew it. Momentarily I turned my head to catch the movements of the horseflies circling above my head. When I returned to the sky spectacle I was astonished to find that the two clouds were gone! There were only two medium-sized clouds near where the original two had been!

From the west shone the sun to illuminate the woodsy border. When the horseflies caused me to fight them off with my sketchbook, I quickly arose and walked briskly around the bend to see what was there—only a group of thorny bushes. Some people would not call this area "picturesque," as it has prolific weeds and many of a certain tree that sheds a feathery seed. They might say the land is too flat with not enough variety in hills or in streams, or it is too hilly without enough relief by flat surfaces. Or there is not enough sunshine, or the color of the leaves is too monotonous, or there are too many bugs, not enough rain, too many shade trees or chipmunks, not enough deer, or . . . or . . . or . . . oh dear! What is it that would enable me to call the landscape "not picturesque"? Perhaps an echo of a cultural concept, an accepted stereotype of landscaping. It is not my aim to discover a "picturesqueness" of nature but its basic simplicity. The lands are lands and nature abounds in them.

Some cedars in the border were perfectly defined from any view. I heard the voice of the same solitary bird that I had heard in the woods more than two weeks ago. Again it was the song of a poet whose lyrics echoed on every tree, penetrating the depths. The wind and trees became an orchestra in the tall rustling grass with the percussion of other birds and insects. And there came the sun to conduct a perfect production. Down in the valley by the community was the lake that townspeople called "picturesque." From where I stood on the road, the lake, barely visible, was reacting with foam on its slapping waves. The lake does have some appeal, even though I happen to know that it is surrounded on all sides by small cabins used by visitors. Although I may have desired to walk to Lake before civilization situated on its shores, I today chose to walk in an "empty" field. Nature itself does not ask that one feel lonely; it just asks for one to be alone. There is a difference.

August 10

I found a path on a hillside covered with high rough grass. I slowly pioneered a trail, leaving thin scratches of wet spears on my legs. I was annoyed at first to find a boxer dog following me. Deliberately gearing my steps into taller grass, I could hear his breathing behind me. The dog accompanied me, not as an enemy but as a traveling companion, letting me make all the decisions as to the direction of exploration. I did not pause too long in any one place; I didn't want to keep him waiting. Occasionally he seemed tempted to pursue the subjects of animal scents, but he remained close by. The dog was silent—not like people—but I could see the depth of tenderness in his face with its huge reddish eyes.

> *Grasp onto the eyes*
> *That view the skies*
> *And world with love*
> *And tears and lies —*
> *The eyes.*
>
> *The meeting is glad*
> *And fair and bad;*
> *The eyes are yours*
> *To see the sad*
> *And mad.*
>
> *The glance is hired;*
> *A current wired*
> *The light of the eyes;*
> *A spark is stirred*
> *And fired.*

Since my aim was to lose the sight of the community, we gradually retreated to the grass-covered hillside, now silhouetted by the sun shining from behind. Climbing to the top, I felt as if the dog and I were coming to the summit of the earth. The hill led down into a valley, which rose into another hill. I thought of running down the hill and then up the hills that followed, letting my hair blow on every side. I chose to walk near the woodsy perimeter with the dog.

A tree in the woods, like many others, tall and limber with abundant healthy leaves, featured lengthy arms that radiated at great distances from the trunk. Their dancing lines crossed each other again and again, and I was reminded of a ballet dancer who repeatedly expresses a recurring theme by her graceful movements. The rhythmic pattern of the branches commanded me to take up my sketchbook, but when I sat down in the grass to open my knapsack, the dog sat on my lap suddenly. I decided to come back to sketch another day when the dog would not be my companion.

We cut back to the undulations of the pasture, great pits into which the earth and sky rolled. Tree clusters accented the pits by extending long shadows into them. The dog breathed hard behind me and, sticking out his tongue, he began to eat some strands of grass. When I patted him, he nudged me, his red eyes revealing that they did not belong to the suspicious types of the community. Dogs are not like the human animal; they can get along very well with the silence. Each living entity is his own detached being, and it is up to each to communicate within himself his significant experience. If I talk about my experience to another man, I'd be telling him the most that I can tell him. But what is truly significant is in my thoughts beyond words. If I had walked with a human, there would be the need to chatter, to fill up space, and the messages from nature on the hilltops and in the woods would be unobserved. The dog combined with nature, and I looked at him with my own thoughts as I look at nature with my own thoughts. It was good to walk with a dog.

With my canine company close behind, I wanted to see what lay on the unseen side of the final hill for the day. Upon reaching the summit, I was again taken at the sight of Lake looming out on the horizon. Since I had always seen it peopled with campers on its shores, I had never really paid much attention to it, but from here the camps were too small to be seen, and the adjacent community was hidden. The bluish-white fog rising from the water was more like a part of the sky that had reached down to take Lake up to it, making it appear more like a shiny white cloud than water. I could faintly see one tip of the lake before reaching the bottom of the hill. The dog had lingered on the hilltop but he now came bounding down at me. Good-bye, Lake. I'm glad we could meet as individuals . . . .

Back in the world of concepts came distractions. Persons in front of the store were eager to lead me to a day of shallow sunlight. Every adornment on the street was a material marker to bring my thoughts to my skin and to the surface. I did not linger in the community and I passed by fishermen on the shore. I enjoyed a silent companion all the way back to camp.

August 14

I found the tree that had recently attracted me with its long and dancing arms. They passed fore and aft another tree — a scrawny, barren pole, white with no arms. The larger tree appeared to embrace a barren tree skeleton. I found some large rocks on which to prop my sketchbook and sketched the two trees, omitting the leaves of the prolific tree to expose the branches and the reaches that nature is capable of. I tried to clear my head of the images of people and the past and pretended that the wind rising in the background was coming to sweep my mind clear. Gradually I escaped from the people who exist in remote communities of memory and imagination as well as in the community nearby.

How quiet it is. How very quiet — these woods where I have come. There are no noises, no concepts, hooting at me, which would not help me today. Nor is there any other individual here trying to convince me with his own interpretation. Even his truth would be noise to me now. How suddenly conscious I become when the gentle sounds, not noise, of Nature embalm me with their own medicine. Such significant experience is like a sweet peaceful rest and yet like an awakening into the place of the soul. My body is a live thing; my arms and my legs, my hair and my skin, are all alive, all mysterious endowments of life! I breathe! Here comes a moment when I acknowledge that I am part of this thing that is Nature. I am aware of awareness and myself as a living being not so different from a living animal or the living ground on which I stand.

On the way back I stopped and looked at my feet mingling with the grass and clover. How impossible it seemed that I had actually passed through infanthood, childhood, and all the stages previous to this one. For it was definite that I had always stood here with my feet mingling with the flowers of the field. My self loomed large as the past and future melted away like the last moments of the sun. And now as I stand alone and alive in the present reality, who listens to the rush of the human soul? Only I can become a union for myself. Only I can be the audience for myself. As I reflect upon the images of Nature, I realize a place is much more vivid after experiencing it a second time. Nature demands familiarity and effort.

CHAPTER | 2

Winding Down Summer

August 17

I spent part of today walking on the railroad track with a ten-year-old boy and his younger sister. We stayed on the track with the boy's agreement to allow me to observe the landscape as we hiked. I found, however, that I could not really observe anything; the talking of especially the boy was unlimited. While he described his cuts and scratches received in an earlier period, nature and its colors were going by. Once or twice, in a lull, I started to engross myself in a tree or rivulet, but I was soon interrupted by the innocent confessionals of the child.

He who wishes to see, find, or discover—really see, find, or discover—must go alone. The attempt may be ridiculed, and isolated tracks may be hard to find. There may be a hundred people ready to offer company. But they are like those who participate in everything, belong to everything, and are close to their skins for lack of sufficient wellspring. Freedom for the individual is release from the others. A man is strong to the extent that he achieves his independence. To be alone is the way.

I had to excuse myself from the children. They were eager to continue walking, but I kindly and flatly refused. I entered a field after assuring myself that they were safely on the way to their home. I wandered about looking for pleasing tree forms, those that afforded likely images for deliberation. A few young trees were evenly scattered about. I noticed a dark hole at the sideline, the entrance to some woods. It looked like a cavern in a wall of light green. I entered the cavern and walked a short path to a little brook. At this moment, I was without a particular name, country, or nation, and I was aware of feeling truly alive.

The interior of the woods was composed of cedars struggling close together for snatches of sunlight. The sparse yellow-green of their tops competed for the opening to the sky. Traces of sun flickered among the leaves and played on the moss and grass by a brook, revealing vibrant color. I blinked my eyes. In the bright intensity I observed green dots hopping about with darker hues of stable background. This was the first time that I had truly seen green. A peculiar thing is nature: it can provoke shades of intense awareness when the image of nature is broken down into elements.

Returning to my rental, I decided to test myself. Sitting on a bed, I began to concentrate as if I were intently observing the fields or the wilderness. Blinking hard, I saw fibers, shadows, colors, and shapes of the table, chairs, curtains, and walls around me. From this I theorize that the human soul, when held back from the environment of nature, attempts to transpose manmade forms into elements of the abstract. It is the soul that begs to be delivered from objects and affairs molded by the masses. It is the soul that, when confined to the room of mass-concepts, compels itself to transform them into essentials for its own contemplation. These may be similar to fibers, shadows, colors, and shapes of the unaffected environment of nature. From these, the soul hopes to reach its own design that survives and stops short of nothingness.

August 22

Against my resolve to not befriend local children, for the last two days I walked with juveniles. The suspicious stares and concealed gossip about me by the townspeople prompted me to attempt acceptance by two boys, brothers aged nine and eleven, who have been my hiking companions. I sometimes reasoned that walking with others, children included, is less conspicuous than walking alone. It was fun climbing to "secret rock" with them and hiking to the place where the huge strawberries grow. I watched them delight in cloud formations and the rocks on the shore of Lake. I listened to their talk about fishing, killing insects, and mashing frogs. I asked them all sorts of questions about themselves and they told me everything, never admitting to not knowing the answers. We went on long hikes through the woods, to the next town, to the lumberyard where their father works. We picked strawberries, explored the attic of an abandoned house, walked dogs through a field. They took me over to their house where I met their mother and five sisters. I also met their uncle who tore up my portrait sketch of him because the similarity was too great.

Having given their approval of me through the enthusiasm on their faces, the boys informed their friends that I was safe to approach. Soon the parents, who had once suspiciously stared at me from their windows and given me a few unfair epithets, ceased to ask me if I were "lost." I was henceforth a member—although a peculiar one—of their community.

Small children are like tadpoles and dogs. They don't cut the trees down. They may climb on them and bend them but they don't saw them down. Furthermore, as a dog views me in terms of his own thoughts to form his canine concept of me, so children do not need the ideas of adults in order to get to know the world and me through their own imaginations. Too soon the individual that is the small child grows into an older child. Later he begins to sacrifice himself to the community. I saw that the boys' oldest sister had abandoned her delight in rocks and her wonder about the heavens to adopt more earthly concerns like cooking and the cleaning activities of her parents, the chaperones of mass-thought. But children—even small ones—are not interested in the discovery of a soul, the kind of soul that brought me here this summer.

It became time to again part from the children to continue my mission. This was hard to do, since children adhere like water to the shore. It was only after a refusal to play when I succeeded in getting them to stop knocking on my door. I hurried like a frightened squirrel past the boys' house on the paved road, but I was spotted by a few other children who had met me recently. As if running for my life, I jumped off the paved road for my own roads in the woods fairly close to "secret rock." I reasoned that soon I may not have the kind of freedom I've had this summer.

At last in the woods again, I saw short red weeds intermingling with the grass and yellow buttercups; stumps were sharing space with cedars, birch, and elm; boulders were implanting the steep hillside. The red weeds were bouncing red dots; stumps were threads of grey fibers; leaves were fans vibrating in the sunlight. I saw that cedars had extensive warty surfaces from which no limbs grew; I heard soaring winds affect the whole woods; I felt crisp outlines of crevices in the old rocks; I witnessed how yellow a buttercup can be. I was no longer located in a specific land, community, state, or kingdom. I was in no particular place—I was merely on the ground. Even the sounds and ruckus of men on a distant pavement did not faze me while I was both nowhere and everywhere in association with nature's elements. First running, then hiding behind a cedar, then running again, I exited, leaving my emergence from the woods unseen. The only person who saw was myself and I was not ashamed.

August 26

I walked on an unpaved road a little way, reaching a grassy area. Huge black horseflies swarmed around my head, distracting me completely. The more I tried to evade them, the more of them were there to attack my ankles. I tried fighting them violently with my hands but they returned immediately. No matter if I stood in the road's middle or off the road, the problem of the horseflies was upon me.

My life is not my own. From the society from which I attempt reprieve, the annoyances of concepts, codes, and industry follow me. I swat at them with my hands but I cannot evade them. I cannot walk through the world without being told how little I am, how insignificant I am. I am told to crush down feelings, to speak someone else's creeds, to smile when the flies of mass-thought prepare to drink my blood. I am expected to speak nothing but a norm, a conventional interpretation of what is established in the world of concepts. I accept it; I follow its code in action. But I do not feel it — it is not part of me — I do not believe it. It is the bite of an insect quite external to my system.

I never did get to think much today — at least not as completely as I would have liked. During an interlude in the harassment by the horseflies, I concentrated on sparkling leaves swaying in a gentle but invigorating wind. Then I saw my shadow alone — as it always is — on the road. Emerging as from a dream, I, the individual alone on the road, became the only being alive and sole ruler of the universe. Thus did I govern eternity at least for a brief and present moment.

A welt on my wrist engaged my attention. I had never really looked at my hand before. My thumb had five prominent lines at the knuckle and little hairs and pores of various widths and lengths. How fantastic and beyond my own understanding was my own thumb! Before I could further pursue these thoughts, the horseflies found me again, drawing my attention to the discomfort of my finite body. I ran away, planning how to rid myself of them once and for all. The rain concluded today's adventure.

August 27

I wandered off the paved road to what used to be woods. Death paced all about this remnant of woods: the lumbermen had been there. Sawed-smooth stumps and arms of pine lay decaying and unburied. Unearthed chunks were exposed to the air; and the moss cover was mashed. White sticks formed matted clusters while rocks showed gouges made by machines.

Nearby was a deserted trailer on wheels that had been used by the lumbermen, probably as their resting quarters. By the entrance, decimated trees were as high as my waist. The entrance had no door. When I climbed up two steps, I met the effects of rust deteriorating the yellow, metallic walls. A long table, mud-filled boots, an automobile passenger seat, and a few cups and spoons were all that remained of the crew who had once fed heartily in a heavy air of perspiration. There were food wrappers wet from exposure to the damp air. Insects canvassed the floor. The persons who shared this trailer earned a living here. I wonder how I should survive in conscience if I had been one of them. Would I have become like an old food wrapper eventually? Looking at the decaying rubbish, I noticed the growling in my stomach as well as hunger for an answer. I abruptly left the place where death had occurred.

I found some woods untouched by lumbermen. The trees were mostly pine and there were birch trees whiter than any cloud. Although the pines had wide trunks and waving branches with dark clustered needles and cones, they grew very close together and sported for the sunlight. In fact, they grew so close together that they looked like they were dancing with each other. The extreme verticality succeeded in sending my eyes to the sky.

I listened to the silence while the wind resonated with deep sighs. The silence was as pure and as sterile as the white bark of the birch trees. An unseen animal tiptoed close by. I looked at the ground, examining some fallen pine needles, and realized that these slender rods were equivalent to the flat and pointed leaves of the deciduous trees. I headed back to the main road. I looked up at the clouds and remembered the question the boy had asked the other day: "I wonder how far up the sky is?" I wonder too. And if it really is infinite.

August 29

I am warm. I have food. I am not lonely. And I am in these woods. All morning, using matches from the world of men, I fed the flames of a little fire in a circle of stones. The fire provided me with a little cooked food, some warmth, and a pleasant place to rest. My fire could have burned ten thousand years ago.

> *Fire, fire like a gipsy,*
> *Blue smoke in the haze,*
> *Tying together all time*
> *Like summer days.*

Society has not only failed to acquaint itself with Nature, but it renounces Nature as out-of-date. I may escape for my Life momentarily but I must always drag my captive feet back to the populace for the needs of my body. Society lashes me with a whip of conformity in events, organizations, trivial duties, and external codes of conduct. Some say that life is action; they do not consider that their lives could be compatible with passive contemplation. Perhaps when they are faced with silence, they retreat, running because they are embarrassed to consider its peace. I would rather my security harmonize with serenity inside of me. In the woods today, at least for a while, the little fire both sustained my body and fed my soul.

It is my desire to think of a society that satisfies needs for body and soul. I want to eliminate preoccupation with things beyond those basic for the body, to discipline society to concern only for food, warmth, and a minimum of things for a comfortable place. I would rather have a box for a table and simple fare along with a bug on the floor than responsibility for too abundant wealth and excessive material things. What could I buy that is more profitable than knowing my inner self in the purest sense? It is my wish to keep nature abounding. It is my need to send forth inspectors of woods, fields, weeds, and trees to find my Self no longer abolished from my home, but restored there. The earnest soul constantly strives to return to Nature.

September 2

Today I looked at a patch of moss. At first it seemed like the usual green mound, but it was more than that. This patch of moss was as complex as the tangle of a whole forest. Networks of green fiber resembling snow crystals intermingled with red-headed pins and tiny white bowls on stems. I shuddered at the thought of the things I could not view with my eye, things about the moss that were on the microscopic level or sensible only to an insect. A white worm no longer than my thumbnail emerged in the middle of the maze. The moss was more than green; it was delicious and frightening.

As I did not create the moss, so I did not create my dark hair, nor the pores and epithelial cells of my skin, nor the five wrinkles on my thumb. Neither did I create the veins protruding on the back of my hand nor the cuticles on the nails of my fingers. What can I not understand about my hand? Everything. What can I find about my hand that is not as intricate and as mysterious as a patch of moss?

As I did not create the size and number of my teeth, nor a young stem, nor the processes that sent me from babyhood into adulthood, so do I not make my own thoughts. As I note the lengths of the lines on my palm, so I note the lengths and breadths of my thoughts. As I scrutinize the shape of my nose, so do I scrutinize the shape of my thoughts. As I do not know when I might find happiness or nostalgia, so I cannot predict the urgent declarations of my thoughts. As I find a shoe to fit the foot I was born to have, so I try to find an environment to fit the birthright of my thinking. As I daily watch the evolution of my body, so do I daily watch the evolution of my thoughts. As I observe the deep bottom of a pond, so I observe the depths of myself: I am the observer of myself.

Beside the mossy mound was a tree no more than a hand high. It had ten tiny leaves in all—but what perfect leaves! Each had three lobes in a scalloped border with each scallop ending in a delicate and slender point. The tiny stem that supported the young tree might grow to be the trunk of an adult tree. It could grow to be the trunk of one of the tallest trees in the forest! As the normal stem grows into a large trunk so I have grown from a baby into an adult. As a small stem cannot alter the processes that change it into a trunk, I have not evaded the processes that brought me into being where I am now.

I do not understand myself as if I were my own creator: I do not control the operations that gave me the body of a human. The most I can do is observe myself as I would an interwoven patch of moss. I am a person; I call myself a person. I work and eat and do all that anyone can. I am the body full; all my cells respond; my health is blessed with the peace of a ripening sun. I am a person—merely a person—with finite power and limited opportunity. I am growing. Each year tiny changes occur in my body as I emerge from the pangs of late childhood. And like my body, my truth grows. From the feeling of being truly alive on the early precipice of my inspiration come new feelings and impressions. I see my growth as from a limber green stem.

Let man discover, if he is inclined, the thoughts given to him in the environment of nature. Let him see the artistry of his thinking as perfectly scalloped as the leaves of a young tree. Let him discover his thoughts as grass on rolling hills or as warbling solitary birds. Let him consider the landscape a medium for revealing his meditations as delightfully tinted as the hills. Let man observe his truth well — sculptured with the help of the genius hand of Nature.

As much as man's thoughts are revealed by nature, art is facilitated by the efforts of man. As an artist, man fashions his truth from nature's images. General and unformed nature is the medium for expressing unique individuality. Yet as much as my own feelings of awe form an expression of me, another's feeling of unseen supremacy is an expression of himself. If he feels in the fabric of the moss the power of an Unseen, who can deny it? Who can disapprove of a feeling that is one artist's expression of growing and developing? While nature has not proven to me that a separate supremacy is at hand in fields and woods, nature has not declared to me for sure that It is not there.

I studied the moss and tiny tree a long time before young squirrels began to play on the forest floor in spite of my presence. I stumbled on the stump of an old tree that had been sawed to death by the lumbermen. Counting its tree rings I discovered it had existed four times as long as I had. Yet it seems I must be alive in a completely different way than was the tree. Before I came to the main road, I found another dead tree trunk in which three young pines had taken root.

September 4

Because the ground was wet from last night's rain, I had some trouble starting my fire, but I kept it going using birch bark as fuel. I sat in a wild plot of flowers. The world of concepts classifies these plants as weeds. If they were weeds, what unusual weeds they were! Among them was a plant consisting of two huge leaves each longer than my foot and wider than the length of my hand. Another was tall and skinny with yellow blossoms. Among some clover was a white plant that twisted and turned like lightning. There were tall stems with knobbed tops that tickled my nose. Small maple and fir trees emerged in the weed pool, peeping at me among leaves of many shapes.

It was a flower garden of weeds! How well they got along without the gardeners of men. Here was enchanting jewelry: delicate green feathers, hairs delicately interwoven. My eyes alighted on the flashy orange of a weed as dazzling as hills in morning. What carefully planned garden would not be enhanced by the brightness of the weed-flower? I can feel about the weed today and the feeling would be true. Yet no matter how differently I feel tomorrow about this weed, I can never call today's feeling false or untrue. The delight I actually feel is true for the moment I have it. I do not separate from the plants I see when defining myself. Men and concepts say "weeds," but I know the plants I saw today were flowers. And I know that on that same plot of ground were plants I didn't see. In time, I could include them in my imaginative moments of experience. For now, I absorb from the ground only the things that I see. If I cannot see, touch, and feel what is nature, how can I reach interpretations of it? I need all of my senses to know myself in nature's landscapes, basic and simple yet delicate and infinitely complex. It is not necessary to plant a garden of special flowers when there are available pleasing weeds. I was delighted by the ones I saw, nameless to me.

September 8

I stayed all afternoon in the woods today in spite of continuing intermittent rain. Not only did my little fire heat up my skin, but my stomach was warmed by coffee from my pan placed in the cinders. Fall is coming. Preoccupied with the fire and securing the shelter of trees, at times I wished that I were tucked away in a warm and soft bed—a conceptual bed in an inviting cottage. I drew my eyes to the swirling, leaning treetops. I heard the thoughts that seemed to come through no decision of mine:

Where the treetops meet the sky
There is eternity.
So states the sky. Yet who am I
To know so boldly?

Only a massive boulder
From out of a dark sea
Observing on the shore
Temporarily.

Eternity may be childishly explained as the union of the separate infinities: the infinity of space, the infinity of time, and the infinity of diminishing size. It seems nonhuman, uninterpreted, imageless, and devoid of the "is" of being. It certainly is mysterious. Furthermore, it actively participates as the doer of itself rather than the aloof observer of itself. Life is a time to rest from the motion of an eternally flowing river.

Eternity does not need consciousness such as I need for consideration of the world. The living consciousness says: "I observe and I am astounded." When I rejoin the unconscious cord of eternity, I shall renew my membership in the state of complete participation in nature. It is the bowing of conscious interpretation to the unconscious and engrossing inactivity of complete knowledge. The wind was generous to grant me the image of the leaves in the treetops, flickering and signaling to me the notion of eternity. I had not come to this part of Nature before. By my small fire in the woods I listened to my own thoughts and wondered at myself.

Many different worlds are made
From one poor earthly ball,
But unified in peaceful shade
When joined in slumber all.

Man, because he is man, ever seeks a conscious picture of the infinite. Only eternity knows the truth of itself, but it knows without consciousness. As man can never explain as if he were their creator, the structure, plan, meaning, and mystery of the forms of nature, I likewise consider eternity without understanding. I am unable to comprehend it. Man ultimately has no more explanation for eternity than he does for nature and himself. His allowed goal is to observe what is here. He is like a prisoner seeking escape from inside the body of an animal. Yet the prisoner himself is a trap, for there is yet a prisoner inside of him.

Man, because he is man, ever seeks to interpret eternity, ever seeks to say of it: "This is." A "this is" of a man cannot hope to reduce the universe into the One lingering interpretation to be accepted by all men. It is fated to remain the interpretation of the one individual. It is but one observation, interpretation, or reaction. It is an individual truth, an agreeable discovery for himself.

Nature asks man to be alone but it does not ask him to feel lonely. Nature asks not that he feel the symptoms of dread isolation; this would only make him want to rid himself of nature's prospects. The sweet images of hills and trees would turn into threats and mockery; the streams, grass, and mountains would turn into mere barriers to love and companionship; the shadows, the suspicious shadows, would only mean something hollow and futile. What man can ever discover his soul all the days of his life without restlessness, without desire of contrast? What man, though he possess an artistic soul like the network of a patch of moss, can travel continuously through nature's paths without some need of food and drink?

My fire had died and I became slightly chilled. A little lonely pang was fired by the mood of the windy and bleary day. The wind of evening blurred the image at the treetops. I reached for a heavy sweater from my knapsack and gathered kindling with which to resuscitate my fire. I decided for coffee again to warm my stomach.

✻   ✻   ✻

The next day I left for New Jersey, flying from Presque Isle to Newark. I hope to return to wooded lands someday to live without interruption. I may stay in civilization long enough to earn what I need to make the move. I wonder which woods? Will I be able to live there alone? Would I need to get a job while living there? Should I try to attract someone to live with me? Is this just a dream that will never materialize?

It is winter now, but I remember summer past. During that summer, I had been in lands where I am known. Nothing could afford me the medicine I need this winter more than the remembrance of my fellowship with nature.

It is a different season now
Than when the leaves were on the bough
Than when they, frolicking in fun,
Adored the passion of the sun.

Existed then a sympathy
For days that blow them from the tree;
But oh! I shivered to behold
Such pretty foliage in mold.

On coming back one month to death,
I found with slender fingers, breath;
For through the valley is the view
I could not see last summer too.

I, standing in a manicured yard, suddenly awakened. My eyes implored the dry leaves and dead grass. The winter air was still. The trees of summer's memory were now stark forms of men and women—quiet people to whom I was related. They swayed with the motions of eternities. I unburied my foot from a shallow layer of snow. In front of me was a long and grey shadow. I knew that I was that shadow of a man, universal man, without name, without trademark, still conscious of life, wonder, senses, and significance. I continued to feel relieved days afterwards by nature's retained images even in the safe, stable, and unconscious world of convention. I try to walk the ways of nature even here.

✳   ✳   ✳

I continued to reflect during the winter and was encouraged by reading. A book of physical geography revealed that people who live in the Arctic zone, where it is perpetually cold, must maintain a constant hardiness and effort. Surely, their preoccupation with the rugged pursuit of food and shelter has sidetracked a more subtle search. The minds of the tropical zone, on the other hand, seem uninspired since the comparable ease of obtaining food, simple clothing, and shelter could leave them under a perennial summer sun. In the temperate zone, mankind is kept stimulated by the necessity of using its ingenuity in summer to prepare for the cold winter months, but the people persist in a drive for excessive material comfort, leaving limited time for peaceful reflection and contemplation.

I considered glaciers and volcanoes, earthquakes and geysers, canyons and plateaus. I became aware of dense tangles of tropical forests and of snowy mountaintops and mirror lakes in northern lands. I learned that at this very moment that I write these words in citified society, another world may exist in the thundering roar of an avalanche far away from human eyes and ears. A chapter on astronomy showed photos of giant stars, spiral nebulae, and space. My mind reeled at the prospect of parts of the cosmos in which my body, if actually in such surroundings, would cease.

The days. The beautiful days. They go by unnoticed, unheeded. While I cannot step into quiet woodlands, I am alienated from myself. The city demands I cooperate and compete with others for my survival. Complex society becomes the place to get ready for Life—the endless, monotonous preparation for Life—and death. Here is the dubious opportunity to prepare for something that never comes.

There is a sound beneath the floor
My ears could not despise;
And then I opened up the door
To see it with my eyes.

I only saw the land which stretched
For countless years around;
And so I went inside again,
Forgetting of the ground.

106

Some think happiness is the goal of life, and that it is achieved by actions of the "I go" variety—variously called I go, I do, I watch, I run, I write, I work, I play, I eat, I wear, I shop, and sometimes, I sleep. A worshipper of "I go" would not say he intends to think during a specified time. The activities of the body, often called "amusements," are diversions turning one's attention away from longer-lived considerations. I return to my house, which is complete with ironing board, kitchen utensils, and television set. The walls are painted turquoise and grey, reminiscent of sky and ground. Shrubs are spaced outside the windows of the porch The patio holds tables with glass tops for dishes of sweet and fattening doodads, while in the living room, a stuffed chair faces a wall where hangs a picture of a sunset in the country, a maudlin tribute to the suspected inaccessible.

I am tired. I put forth years of my life in working for "some day." But when my workday releases me from a long, long day, I pick up my fork, my broom, or my rag. Or drive to an empty frolic of unhappy laughter. Or I draw my bath water or take up my book. Or lie on the sofa peering out a window with monstrous plans to escape. Or I dream on.

The solitary breaths we find
Among the others of the blind
In life are few but offering
A golden plate with Life upon it.
The multitude is sooner with us
With men, machines, and everything
Philosophies now do and seem.
We live just then when all is gushed together
On the mind producing strife,
Banality in dress. Trifles snare us
From our birth, mistaken worth.
And we are dying from
The dusty breaths for sure until
The solitary breaths we find
Within the cloisters of the mind
Remake us pure and leaving room

For not a city or a care;
And leave the blistered hands and body both
The tall, the dark, the limp, the stoop
Of Life itself to breathe upon us there.

CHAPTER | 3

Society of Nature

I am modern man, newly returned from my Maine awakening, the first of my species in the society of man, the government of nature. But I still live in the government of the animals of the past. I find no easy adjustment; I am in constant conflict with the concepts here. I am often seen wandering apart from the multitude. Although mass-thought considers me peculiar and strange, I nevertheless tolerate the discomfort of being misunderstood. My inspiration is worth more to me than relief from public concern. I am modern man, secret charter member of a society of the future, for Nature and man.

Society — The government of man is divided into sections of land separated by vast wildernesses. No section reaches the population of some of the metropolises in the history of animal-men. The average section contains no more than five hundred people or as many as are needed for a functioning unit. Each man and each woman residing in the state of nature has betaken himself to his or her own cabin, wherein each abides alone in the woods removed from the sight of other cabins and their inhabitants. Each adult has been issued a plot of land beside his cabin, on which to grow crops vital to his maintenance. As much as possible, each capable adult produces his own food according to his own needs at his own station without borrowing the labor of any other.

Each section is guided by several councillors whose headquarters are a university in each section. Councillors are dedicated to educating, not ruling. They are disposed to counsel, not direct, having little power laid down by written or spoken doctrine. Trust and faith in the councillors suffice to bring harmony. The university functions as the foundation of education and the seat of the government in each section.

Only enterprises that are vital are in effect, such as procedures of planting and harvesting, clothing, housing, utilities, and basic health. As the original monetary system is replaced, the government includes an organized system of barter and trade. Tools used in making utilities for the common good, such as electricity and water, are kept within the premises of the university, while farming stays outside university boundaries. The number of farmers is as large as the count of the healthy adult population. The elimination of both the gross in population and unnecessary material enterprise, a double process requiring hundreds of years to succeed, mark the fall of the original political structure and the freedom of souls to connect with nature.

Many paved roads are cut away and abandoned. Where once there were large cement, wood, and steel buildings of commerce now only trees grow naturally, and nowhere is any pristine area of land degraded except by vital necessity. Vital necessity does not include the chopping or tearing of wild plants to build roads, stores, or overhead utility wires. Natural growth is rarely torn down for the mere sake of sunlight, for the riddance of pollen or feathery seeds, for ornamental or cultivated plants, for pasture land, or for other purposes of unoccupied space. Wood is employed only for the construction of the university building and its systems, and for cabins and their simple furnishings and utensils. Leftover wood fragments are used for the warmth of firewood.

The new society preserves creatures that roam the landscapes. No animal is destroyed or injured for flesh eating or for any other purpose except in the case where the elimination would save the life of a man. The portioning of flesh of animals for the sake of savoring their taste has been denounced as gluttonous, cruel, and unnecessary for the well-being of man. Where husbandry of animals for meat and manufactured products originally existed, the state of man gradually rids itself of the responsibility for these items by non-breeding. Primarily those animals that afford the necessary dairy products for mankind are bred and fed.

Man does without the olive. He lives adequately from plain fruits, vegetables, grains, and dairy products without the ado of elaborate cooking. A wealth of protein may be had from beans and dairy foods. Man grows vegetables according to his liking on his own allotted land, while a common fruit grove provides for all. Men who raise animals for their tax obligation deliver dairy products to the state, which then issues them to the people. Occupied only by that which is necessary, man has rid himself of activity that would take him from his own contemplation. He takes care not to grow more food than his own space allows, since as history shows, extravagant society begins with an excessive food supply.

Taxes — Aside from farming for his own needs, each man contributes a tax for the welfare of the whole government. This tax is a portion of time spent in bodily labor and/or in the contribution of certain items produced by that labor. The construction of cabins and the university with its facilities is necessary. Time is spent in printing, cloth weaving, well digging, establishing electrical facilities, and fabricating implements for scientific research. Other objects needing cooperation for their construction include needles, pins, buckets, soap, musical instruments, art supplies, clay jars, basic tools, and devices for the control of births. There are specialized crops to be provided by a few for the sake of the others. A tax is paid by providing food for the councillors who

111

serve in the guidance of the state. Another tax is paid by caring for the aged and occasionally children. In return for each person's tax contribution, the state entitles him a portion of the product or service of all the occupations contributed as taxes. Each man and each woman is required to participate in the physical occupations as long as they are capable. Men change labors periodically so that all might achieve an integrated and equal exposure to the knowledge of the functioning of the state.

Time spent in labor leaves ample room for contemplation. It is suggested that no more than two and a half hours daily (using the time symbols of my ancestors) be spent in one's own farming and in the tax of labor in the summer. No more than three hours are consumed in personal and community responsibility in fall. In the past, the typical man-animal sacrificed eight hours a day, year-round, to his occupation; consequently, he had little time left to pursue his foundation in thought. In the new state, man preserves his body, the gateway to the mind, by the actions of the body in shortened periods of work. The result is time wherein he has "nothing" to do. Yet as the true man knows, his leisure time is not a place for stupefaction before the next labor; he considers it the time to undertake his real work, his Life's work.

Education — Education does not purport to lead one to material reward or to employment in technical application. In the days of the materialists, hordes were found to be "educating" themselves in colleges training them in business administration, marketing, and industrial studies. Pursued now are the study of the one language, the sciences, historical studies, mathematics, philosophy, literature and the arts, and theory of simplification and preservation of the landscape for the evolved man and his government.

The university is educator and head of state in each section. The university assists and guides each person throughout his lifetime. Each university building also contains facilities for research in the pure sciences and simple medicine, facilities to implement electrical energy, looms to provide clothing, a workshop for study of water access, a storage place for tools, areas for messaging the universities of distant sections, and equipment for

112

printing books to impart the stimulus of education. The government affords to produce its electrical, weaving, telegraphic, water access, printing and other functions as quickly and as simply as possible so that the men of the government might not dwell upon these things but concentrate on more important matters of their minds.

Councillors — Councillors are instructors and guides of the evolved state. Approximately two councillors per hundred are in service in each section. Councillors encourage each student to discover for himself his own thoughts and conclusions from nature and from the areas of instruction. Councillors give voice to matters that separate the state of man from the condition of animal-men.

Councillors:
   a. Uphold the lands everywhere and work for the education of and service to the Government of Abounding Nature. They do not expect fame or material advantage. They do not govern but guide; they have no more rank than the majority of men.
   b. Hate enacting laws and limitations. They are in their hearts convinced that no man of the state is apt to commit deliberate wrong, nor is likely to be dishonest or to avoid virtue. Councillors assume that each individual is directed primarily through his own integrity in the love of the mind's solitude.
   c. Devise, when appropriate, a few reminders to prevent the temptation of man. Some of these reminders will concern registered marriages, the requirement that all capable persons pay their tax, and the policy that no material property be removed from the state. Councillors are makers of peace, ready to solve conflicts with consideration and impartiality.
   d. Project honesty and fairness in their dealings, while deserting the vain and pompous parade of faddish group thinking.

e. Employ kindness of attitude to assuage any difficulties or upsets that sometimes, although rarely, beset the true men of the state. Councillors are makers of peace, always ready to solve conflicts with consideration and impartiality rather than with hostile retaliation. A councillor is outwardly strong, assuming the role of paternalist when one or several sons of the state temporarily become weak sons. Councillors take into private conference those members of the state who need reminding that the government is the state of moral men who operate without laws and who control themselves by looking beyond greed. Councillors desire not to punish, but to reach understanding. They are convinced that education — not laws or threats of retaliation — is the salvation of the state. Councillors recommend eliminating weapons of defense.

f. Possess general knowledge of all the known studies, function as guides in one or several areas, and concentrate on the collected data of one of the sciences. All councillors specialize in the philosophies of general theory.

g. Adopt new methods of teaching. In the past, animal-men were considered educated if they could repeat. The "repeaters" reiterated in detail from books the objective phenomena of science, the shallow circumstances of history, and the conclusions of loud men. Repeaters were not sensitive enough to hold their own convictions, relying on the conclusions of others to fill themselves. Councillors encourage independent thought and the search for the meaning of man and animals in the universe.

h. Conduct small classes enabling individual attention according to the capacity of each student. No student is designated as an example for the others to follow. Each student is offered attention according to his capacity. Councillors hold frequent individual discussions with their students, allowing reticent students and outwardly verbal students equal opportunity. Written reports of student progress are not given, lessening competition among students that could lead to maladjustment of the true purpose of learning. If students prefer, they may be encouraged to take tests given to recruits for special councillors-of-science or practical assistants in occupations—such as water, electrical, and weaving— requiring special abilities or physical prowess.

<u>Induction of the Councillors</u>—Providing there is an opening available, the man or woman, having reached a minimum age of thirty and desiring to be a guide of the government, may arrange a meeting with an incumbent councillor. Since a councillor represents a leader (although a passive one) and the student represents a follower, there could still be the sense of the superior and the inferior. Care is taken to conceal both identities at the meeting. The two parties are separated by a screen during the discussion so that the body and face of each is concealed from the other. The councillor initially presses the contingent recruit in matters dealing with truth and general theory, matters requiring no preliminary study of books. The potential inductee should not plan or rehearse his responses; declarations should be spontaneous and sincere. When a discussion has been completed, the contingent recruit may, if he wishes, schedule another discussion with a different councillor later. Again the bodies and identities of the two are concealed while the discussion focuses on the best that can be in the life of man. Possible inductees or anyone may schedule discussions with councillors.

If the recruit has not abandoned the discussions after a year's time, and if he has spoken with several councillors, the councillors themselves may gather together and vote by ballot to approve or disapprove an identifying number of the candidate. There is nothing discussed by the councillors about any candidate before the time of the voting; each vote must represent a councillor's private thought which is not influenced by others. The incumbent councillors choose the succeeding councillors of the state not for a candidate's external charm of talk but for the depth and sincerity shown. The councillors do not look for leaders, but for guides; not for popularity of the boisterous and the talkative, but for depth; not for attraction of beautiful bodies, but for the beatific spirits of minds. These, endowed with the propensity for their own souls and virtue, are the likely recruits for the councillors of the government.

The new initiate shall have studied diligently the courses of instruction, including in depth at least one of the sciences. He shall love the true, the good, and the sincere. He shall want to go out into the environment of nature for the knowledge of his soul. He shall not look for any honor of his position; he shall regard it as an opportunity to keep man evolved from the animal-man. He is urged to come a little way from his individual hiding places to help guide the philosophy of man. When he circulates among men, he does not stress practical ends or empty regulations but reveals some of his own philosophical thinking.

A councillor may take on his post for three years or for a term to be decided at the time of selection. If he wishes after his term to return to his own planting and harvesting, or to seek relief as a student himself, he may do so. Some citizens may desire to explore the solitude of nature more than they would ever aspire to be guides and educators of the state. In the government of man, all may be students, including the councillors. Members of society often need the boost of education throughout their lifetimes. The education of man invites all persons of all ages to participate.

The Areas of Instruction
1. Language: Grammar and usage of one language.
2. Basic Sciences: Geology, bacteriology, chemistry, biology, botany, and geography. The sciences require consideration of their practical as well as non-practical significance.
3. Animal Sciences: Zoology, anatomy, biology, and the science of evolution. These sciences tend to collect and to classify phenomena. An appreciation of the integrity of the lives of animals is a welcomed benefit.
4. Electrical and Water Sciences: These studies consider philosophical implications as well as ways to use resulting products for the state.
5. Astronomy and Space: There is much room for philosophical interpretation from spatial description.

6. Historical Implications: This study is a review of the events, customs, and movements undergone by the stock from which man evolved, from the struggle for the barest necessities to the conflict against the excess of materialism. It is not merely a long story of the shifting and doings of bodies. It does not memorize the dates of wars, the colors of uniforms, or the amendments to laws. Significance is found in the motives, meanings, and implications of past events.
7. Mathematical Theory: The study of mathematical theory not only considers the practical applications of basic mathematics, algebra, geometry, and related studies, but it also considers philosophical implications. It asks if numbers in themselves are impersonal and how they relate to zero and infinity.
8. Art: Art forms, including the musical, performing, pictorial, and plastic, are not scrutinized much for their composition or their method of construction but for the meanings which they evoke in the artist's self-understanding. Art's purpose is not primarily for communication. If art is sincere and full of the individuality of the artist, it will be satisfying to the artist without an examination by others. Art is concerned with important meaning to that person, and it is to be deemed an activity next to the primary importance of individual contemplation. As individuals have different feelings when confronting the same woods or field, likewise men feel differently when beholding or listening to the same artwork or production.

Music, involving composers, performers on instruments, and perhaps singers and dancers, could allow composers and performers to call up their own thoughts and images as a result of the promptings of synchronized chords and rhythms. Singing and dancing, although not frequently performed in the state, have some value to the performer if there are few other performers singing and dancing simultaneously, if he is in sympathy with the accompanying music, and if the production has not been extensively rehearsed. The singer or dancer may thus express his thoughts in synchronization with the musical promptings.

Secondarily, the audience at a musical production may benefit from both communication from the composer and from their own thoughts stimulated by the musicians, dancers, or singers.

In the performing art of drama, not one member of a cast can freely act due to the restrictions on his individuality imposed by the plot interaction. Some value of the dramatic arts lies in their ability to communicate to others meaningful and felt emotion, but if the actor is not expressing his own individuality, if he is merely fused with others, reduced value is left for him even if it were possible that all in the audience could receive the same message intended by the author of the performance material.

Pictorial and plastic arts encourage sketching, painting, and sculpture. I make pictures. Yet if I have no strong feeling for the images I capture, if I see little significance in the landscape, then why record them with pencil or paint? If my expression does not sound loud in my mind, then the picture is a draft of emptiness.

Art in painting of pictures includes images of the landscapes of nature and of the animals and men situated in those landscapes. Art in pictures could also include as subject matter, although to a lesser degree, the equipment associated with the basic needs of man, the scientific researches, the facets of the university building, farming activities, cabins, and other appliances in the society of nature. If pictorial art does not incorporate recognizable images, then it usually tries to isolate in abstract patterns and shapes the feelings once associated with the actual images. Any art is valid that captures the soul, which, in accord with the artist's feelings, individualizes from the universal environment of mankind. Even pictures by the original animal-men showed infant stages of true art: few cars, billboards, television sets, or store interiors were portrayed because they were concepts far removed from universal images of nature and basic society. The fact that most pictorial art by the original animal-men did not include some elements of their complex society shows that even then art tended to the natural.

Because the function of art is to bring the soul outward, there should be no restriction as to type of medium, composition, or subject matter within reason. In the days of our ancestors, weighty rules for composition and style directed and propelled the concepts of rigid craft. Since any work is valid that satisfies an individual as the record of his true feeling, the tendency to judge works as "good" or "bad" has been eliminated and the giving of prizes to the "best" works has been discarded. Works to be exhibited are taken at random from works particularizing from universal views of nature and society. The communication of souls is not a competition.

9. Philosophy and Literature: Philosophy is a frank admission of inner conviction about the meaning and goals of Life. Literature which comes straightforward in nonfiction reveals individual feelings without dwelling on the structure, plot, and resolution of the presented material. Fiction stories, so often employed by animal-men for extravagant detail and compelling adventure, have been discarded in the state of man.

Of the forms of communication, the written word as nonfiction—sincere, unhesitating, and revealing—comes closest to the harbor of individual expression, ready to shed every kind of garment the soul may wear as it wanders through the forests of itself. Not attempting to evade it, literature tries to pinpoint the soul. It is thought alone in the minds of individuals that is the reality. Although a man may pour out his soul in words, he has only told of it; he has yet to reveal it. His soul vibrates to the strings of internal feeling; it can never really be known by any other man through communication; it is the individual's alone. Authors do not need elaborate acceptance by biased publishers who thrived in the past.

10. General Theory: Theory is the most vital study in the educational program. It teaches that modern society must be limited in organization and in functional industry for simplicity's sake. No man need graduate from theory; with its consideration he may ever consider infinite pathways.

I take up a newly dug potato in my hand, searching for cuts in its skin, and observe that nothing is as it appears to be! How did this potato end up in my hand from where it germinated in a field? Is it a Maine or Idaho potato? A result of science or Source? I am molded in a terrific insecurity of which my very self is a part. Theory helps acceptance of the knowledge that the scenes of the cities of the last age, which used to command my faith, my security, have fallen away, rightly leaving me to bravely bear the fact of the mystery of everything, including the last ounce of myself. I am the mere observer of myself.

Possessions — A person calls no object his own. His cabin of two small rooms contains an oven for heating and cooking, a bed, table, chairs, refrigerator, and lighting equipment. A well may be dug for water. Electrical equipment and furniture are constructed for, and not moved from, cabins. The allotted land for each house includes a simple plow, shovels, and other utensils for the efficiency of farming. Not with the coming and going of men are any of these things taken away.

Homes of my ancestors contained ashtrays and bowls, glass, china, brass trophies, radios, television sets, record players, and irons. They housed four chairs when only two were needed and two tables when one was sufficient. They contained magazine racks, potted plants, newspapers, recreation rooms, and swimming pools. They displayed paint on the walls and caged birds. When departing from a residence, my ancestors would carry with them their heavy ordeal of furniture, lugging it from place to place. They would rub against their possessions, bump against them, catch themselves on splinters. Soon they would feel the terrible stretch of their muscles demanding rest, and they would yield to the furniture, quenching desires to venture forth to consider important things.

Regarding possessions in the new society, man yields to the moths his torn clothing, especially residual party clothing; he throws into a creek that extra store of water that would surely bear mold anyway; he takes out of his food area those petrified nuts and buries them in the ground for strengthening the soil; he dismantles his ancient robes and relishes, wares and earthen statues. But he does none of these things before he has given his accumulation to those who by undesirable circumstances have not come to the point of having the basic requirements. He might first give his extra food to that skinny dog he has seen or to those who deem it more of a suffering than a comfort to exist without these remnants of material sustenance. Man seeks to help those who earnestly try to help themselves.

<u>Romantic Joining and Friendship</u> — In the new state, the draw of men and women to each other confuses and inhibits a few of the people who listen to the urge to marry and procreate. This urge, undoubtedly inherited from their animal ancestors, can push individuals into a partnership that usually involves trivial responsibility, stifling togetherness, loss of privacy, a cloister of children, and what is most disastrous to the individual, a forgoing of the pursuit of inner convictions. What an urge it is to yield; to caress one another in a cloak of external disguises; to beget, to be surrounded by automatic companions in order to forget for the moment the awful mortality of the body and the loneliness of the individual within it!

Who really are they to be born? Are they not little bodies of security to soothe the aging fears of the parents? Are they those who would choose to remain unstirred in eternity? Children are desired not for the sake of granting the unborn the privilege of undergoing the world that comes with their birth. Instead, the bodies of offspring are brought forth to demonstrate the struggle for existence besetting the parent. See how the little ones depend on him, tax him, spend him, consume the leisure of him. See how the babes gather round and clasp him with gentle and warm arms. See how they laugh — they effervesce — and applaud the one who, without knowledge of how creation can possibly perform, gave them breath and shape. See how these extensions of the flesh enhance the parent, obscure the loneliness threatening the animal in him, prolong the security of his pathetic existence, call him superior and excellent. Who will listen to the cries of the yet to be?

A child born in the state of man lives part-time with each parent until he reaches adulthood, whereupon he acquires his own cabin. Children are urged to associate with the university and matriculate in it at ages appropriate for each individual. The Society of Nature seeks not to grow in population.

If these living plants that we call people
Were suddenly told to stop reproducing,
They would have nothing to live for;
Their hands in the balmy breeze of day
Reach for anything to cling to,
Anything for support.

Weak people, weak plantlike people,
Lean on their children,
Who in turn lean on theirs, and theirs, theirs.

The true man earnestly discourages the urge of procreation even as he yields to it; he gives birth to the Life of his own mind before he surrenders to produce the bodies of children. While the true man struggles to hold down the creature vestiges in him, he is not separate from the creatures; his world is the same natural world as theirs and he is governed by the same natural urges. He is not apart from the wild and domestic animals, but he continually prepares to be.

Friendship involves real importance, but it is not preferred for the reason of the second person. But where is this friendship, and who in the animal states had it — and yes! — who in the state of man? Even here does the mere feeling of loneliness push some into relationships to fill a void. How often does an individual yield his independence, his struggle for his own convictions, to a stifled togetherness? Rarely is painful isolation quenched from the attempted unity of two or more persons merely associating together, compromising quiet environment for the individual.

The role of man is to be alone. To pursue his Life, he must be apart from others. Solitude is his condition. All other conditions, including the presence of wonderfully stimulating companions, are mere antecedents to the solitude that precipitates satisfaction. Having left the crowd, the womb of babbling unconsciousness, man intuitively knows that the truth of his own consciousness would be better. Now more than ever comes the realization that no one can be alive for him; no one can interpret the world for him; no one can die for him. True man traverses the world little published to others, while leaving the shouting and external animal-men-of-action to applaud themselves in noise. A true man is not upheld by society's conformity.

The true man is leery of those who seem to be his friends. Man, having stooped a while to search for friends and finding none, shall not despair but shall rise to independence and self-sufficiency. He shall desire not the burden of false companions for mutual borrowing and begging, for wasting his time and delaying significant life. "Small talk" is the agreement of the outer crusts of parties, but only foppery and affectation may emanate. The true man, friendless and apart from the crowd, knows a pain and insecurity, but he endures and welcomes them as preludes to finding his individuality. He withstands separation and departures from the companions of his childhood, preferring meaningful exposure to meaningless togetherness. Man finally realizes that friends to him are not mere bodies with which to surround himself but those who share similar inner convictions, who have surveyed the world and arrived at a similar worldview. Friends are like states of mind. Upon finding someone who holds similar felt convictions, a man is attracted in proportion as he is attracted to his own convictions.

But how often does the true man realize that friends for him rarely pass his way. How often has he searched for himself in another and found not his own conviction but a contradiction to himself. How often, upon deep investigation, has he found that those that he thought shared his thinking are full of variant and vacant words. How often does man walk singly, knowing that friends for him do not occur except in a rarity (a wonderful, reinforcing rarity).

Feeling alone is not the same as being alone. He rises by himself over the unlikely alliances and circumstances he encounters. Instead of yielding to smothering relationships, he chooses to remain his own guide and friend and to be little known except to himself. His stars and poetry do not desert him. The true man having arrived at himself can hardly disclaim himself, the suffering that comes from within himself, to return to the gaiety and frivolity that obscure self-knowledge. He usually goes to his death anonymously.

<u>In the Event Man Meets Man</u> — By my very birth I was given to a society of brothers who fed and sheltered me. They kept me warm; they preserved my infant body so that now, as an adult, I proceed to discover who I am. Like every other man, I still need. I still must insist on food and raiment and warm shelter. Without the society of brothers I would surely die. And, in order to contribute to the body of mankind, I must consider the prospect of offspring, although with great trepidation.

Basic needs I cannot avoid before I continue to Mind. I am obligated to a cooperation to maintain the body of man and mankind. Man has quit his competition and now practices harmony with others. Man has chosen not to challenge them but to work with them, not to argue with them but to join them, not to look upon them as a threat to his property but as the keeper of it. Since the new society does not desire excessive portions and since it is a cooperation upon which each depends, man works to assure that there is no lacking of basic needs for all members of society, while avoiding accumulation acquired by greedy or lustful practice.

Virtue is man's art of keeping the collective body of mankind alive through cooperation and empathy. Virtue is inherent and diffused in society's very network and is rarely brought to temptation or hoarding. An evolved man must always carry his higher man with him; the subtle distinguishing of virtue from non-virtue is constantly considered in the event man meets man It performs with all men. Never shall I, having controlled by virtue my animalistic inheritance, look at one man to conspire that I shall not do any virtuous deed for his need, since he is this particular man. I shall operate for the good of all men, distinguishing not among individuals. Man is full of compassion and empathy, helping a man toiling with his task if the task itself is beneficial. Virtue defends the tormented, the misunderstood, and the misinformed and does not present greed, tyranny, revenge, duplicity, irresponsibility, intolerance, or insincerity. A policy of acting as if others were equal to oneself is a goal of virtue. Virtue sympathizes even with those whose past contains multifarious wicked deeds.

When individuals are their own overseers of honesty and responsibility, the less are the laws and rules of conduct that bound and herded the animals in the age of materialists. Such laws and rules only confuse and obstruct the growth of individuals. Individual morality in the state of man promotes easy agreement among individuals, hastening their departure from one another. The flexible attitude of harmony is a means to the goal.

Virtue pardons those who are temporarily overcome by their lesser selves. Often the clamors of the body precede the manly characters of moderation and reason, and for a moment a man may be distracted and led away from honesty and innocence of mind. Virtue's obligation is to review the underlying motives of questionable behavior of others and to permit forgiveness and second tries. It is not in virtue to aggressively retaliate but to restore peace and harmony. Virtue does not abandon hope when it observes wicked acts. Virtue likes to guide those who are ignorant and to give them further opportunities.

Virtue prefers to fight evil with quiet reach rather than with open revenge. It teaches by subtle words and firm example. Since evil is often firmly set and slow to upset and change, virtue proceeds cautiously and hesitates to use loud characteristics of attack, for fear of becoming evil itself. It tends to subtly react with guidance, but it will use force by hand, not weapons, to curtail evil. Never shall I, having tried guiding and gently transforming the animalistic word or deed, crawl away meek. Someone may talk about me, thinking he injures me with his words, but if he is talking against the appearance, possessions, or movements of my body, then he has left me — the core of me — untouched.

In order to initiate a speedy separation from co-citizens without lingering contact, I approach them with the honesty, good cheer, and general morality characterizing virtue. In short, I practice the upright life with those about whom my mind tells me to "be done." As far as laws that command me and coerce me, the loud protest against which would execute me, imprison me, or hamper the freedom I need to promote change, I proceed by a slow, careful, and subtle operation rather than a sudden outburst. While I externally abide by rules, I am all the while nourishing a policy of change and eventual removal of the nuisance restrictions.

There are some practices that are so obviously full of evil, excess, and disease that they demand my immediate and forceful opposition in spite of consequences. When I catch sight of intolerable evil or indulgence, my obligation is to protest, to opine. My words may be subtle and quiet but they must nevertheless speak. I take risks. At no time do I consent to permit virtue to yield to evil or moderation to excess. When pushed for an honest confession of myself, I do not pretend to advocate exploitation of man or nature. I am ready to suffer consequences rather than yield, risking opposition to codes and concepts not in keeping with my philosophy. Whether or not my opposition takes the form of a retreat, subtle approach, or furious battle, I never permit degradation without my input. In the last resort, the attack against selfish actions shall rise like a whiplash downward to show its true strength, and it shall bruise evil's coarse hide.

The reactions I have to this old society reflect my revelation. I shall not patronize things I do not need. I aspire to no more than food, clothing, and simple shelter for my body without excess. Avoiding luxury business and economics, I choose an occupation close to the ground and relating to food, clothing, simple shelter, farm labor, utilities, and care for the sick, dying, and often for children. Farm labor provides exercise for the health of my body by planting, maintaining, and harvesting vegetation.

I play parts, always temporary ones. I try not to become stagnant in a permanent and particular facet of employment for remuneration. Since I do not resign myself to a permanent avenue of mercenary livelihood, I am largely exempt from the dependence on custom, convention, law, and dogma. The basic occupations that relate to the ground enable me to survive.

Should my whole life's business be of virtue? Surely, in the moments when all my obligations with men have been decently and successfully accomplished, and there is no longer any need for cooperation, when the bodies of men have their physical needs acquired and when I have opposed evil, it is time to return to the harbor wherein no other man resides. Here my self is neither goodness nor badness, and I leave virtue to those whose turn it is to interact with men in the interest of society.

My life goes deep, very deep. Little days and little people confront me with their little ways; little conversations; petty concerns over daily affairs, food and family; efforts at amusement; and their practical futures. But though I may act a little timid, inhibited, and concerned among them (for the mere fact that I must survive among them), I know that I am a mere shadow among them—a mere body—and that I am known only during times when I have quit their concerns.

Time is tasks to people some
To one it is the beauty come.

Conclusion

We come a long road. I came a long road. As my past parades before me, I see that I am at present no more than a stage that necessarily waited until now to reveal itself. Before this time I could not think, and only until I became a man could I search to know the man that I am. As the child drifts across my memory so, too, does the person that I was yesterday show me where I used to be. Today I am a new man, and I am stronger as I develop my whole being intensely in connection with the natural world. Yet as maturity is a fraction and shall not last, my thoughts are not fixed and I shall not stay where I am now.

What is this that I see, that I surmise of myself, lovely and flushed in the age of true man? What is this thing that, like an ax, chops at myself, at my philosophy, recklessly knocking down my society of abounding nature and man? It is of the nature of man. Man. A being trapped in his own being. Destined for reasons of his certain parents, of his certain birth in a certain time and place. Destined from the moment of birth — actually, from long before — and this birth is no more than the delivery of the very young and impressionable body and mind, both of which secretly housed definite tendencies to emerge within environments already set in place, but not yet showing.

With birth, the environment controls a baby's feelings and his feelings control the environment. From the influence of the first environment, the infant "learns" as allowed by his inborn nature.

This is enough to direct his "decisions" in the second environment that is automatically emerging, whether an environment of tangible fact or of state of mind. Moving onward, outward, the child becomes a man, seemingly powerful and independent, but he is man and where he is now by reason of his first environment interacting with his first little mind and body, which had resources for responding to that environment. Man, still learning, still reacting to the succeeding environments, which he seems to motion into view, has an assured fate and is no more unbound than his appearance at birth. He continues on and on, feeling the reward or pain from every one of his actions.

Man, animals, plants, and the heavenly objects in their orbits cannot behave any differently except through illusion. All of the past was inevitable. All of our tomorrows are sure to be known according to law; they already exist in waiting. The cosmos is like an electrical unit with all its parts subordinate to order and mechanism. Man's body cannot be other than it is, due to the physical inheritance to be developed and destroyed with time and place, which he only appears to control.

I cannot be other than I am; the universe cannot be other than it is. It is the scheme for me to have come to this present stage, to have me take the type and depth of the breath that I now inhale, to have me write this very sentence. It is the scheme that I am man. And it is the scheme that there is animal-man. The animal-man's gaudy and materialistic cities are and were inevitable. It is the plan that nature be shut away by dusty buildings, that cars fill paved streets and infect through diseases of roaring and rushing. It is the scheme that these cars contain persons who go nowhere. It is the fixed story that the age of materialists should forget the sky, the trees, the patches of moss, the wonderful simplifications, and the soul's aspiration for the universal. It is the scheme that I am a seer—a man alone and separated from my people. It is the scheme for animal-men to pass me on the street, for them to dislike and ignore me. It is the scheme also to have me think that it is the scheme, and it is the scheme for others to believe that there is no scheme. It is the plot that, as a man isolated from men, I must try to alter the ways and patterns of mass-thought.

Similarly, I attribute the failure of my influence by reason of the predestination.

Predestined, yet unaware of the future. Proceeding to a goal already prepared, but operating under the illusion that something called "I" bears the responsibility for the decisions leading me to it. All I can do now is ride along with the part of me that feels the strain, pain, and cause of every change. All I can do is continue to be the observer of myself, my body, my actions, and my words. At least I have the satisfaction of discovering the character that is decidedly the scheme that I am, that I have to be.

I observe myself. I would seem to form my own thoughts of myself. But surely I do not create my thoughts as I do not create my arms and legs. I move my arm, but what is this arm that I move? I think I am no cause of it! And I wonder how my thought enables the arm to move! I still try: I still seek to know by myself. But the pattern is circular, even the sentence, even the silence. I think I observe freely and impartially but I know I observe myself by necessity. Time already knows every one of the secrets that remain in my mysterious, pathetic, and inevitable drama, already programmed.

I speak to those who are like me. My words of meaning rush only to the ears of those who have ears for hearing, who have already the faculties for receiving the same philosophy. I cannot change those whom I most want to change; I cannot influence anyone who is not similar to me. The willingness to seek nature is bred in my bones. Others are born to perpetually contrive to take and to gain in material advantage to the extent that the whole point of the government of nature is ignored and deteriorating into that original state that places no value on simplicity. The councillors who were to be the finest examples of manhood, who were to be the strongest souls, who were to be earnest guides for individuals of the new state, now fall to the ranks of the mediocre. They have revolted after long subjection to the restraints of the university and have returned to their bodies; they are breeding readily and maintaining themselves by clustering together once again in an age of creature conformity. The new mediocre men are proud to recommend to their children that they be prolific begetters of materialists to replace those who have disappeared.

After all, it is the Absolute for which I really search, for which I have wearily transgressed nature, for which I have quietly but firmly sent up prayers with the smoke of summer fires. It is the Truth of all men and animals; all fishes, insects, and birds; all trees and shrubbery. It sings aloud in the structure of the clouds and in the interior of the earth. It is the one significant sign, the summary of all involvement, pastime, occupation, passion, and reasonable contemplation. It is the answer to mortality, the reason for struggle, the purpose for existence. It is the Truth that makes no exception, that admits no disturbance, no petty contradiction to itself. It is the conclusion of all observation, the Goal that leaves a man no longer the mere observer of himself, but like the creator of himself: real, abiding, and counting the stars. I would like for it to be one Word, a simple answer to all mystery, acceptable by all.

What I seek may lie outside my limited human terms, my shallow finite terms. Human beings may be aware of only one particular kind of universe. Perhaps there are other universes or existences or a different form of time that other kinds of minds know. Perhaps there are other more knowledgeable universes overlapping but invisible to this human one. Surrounded by the universes that I cannot comprehend, that I cannot see, I remain as a raindrop in a forest fire, trapped and insecure, inconsequential and stupid.

As I am brought to misunderstand nature and as I may not approach the boundaries of the Absolute, so may I not fall back to scenes of shops or even to the wooden sides of a simple cabin. My penetrating eye regards any society as appearances, concealing the living ground of Nature, which is the source. From my perspective, the materialistic and conventional scenes of society fade. My conclusions draw as from the heart of life's landscapes.

On the day, on the very day, of my death
I saw all the things of nature very clearly.
I saw the sky with its red lines
Ever floating against the horizon.
I saw the wind, which whistled through me
The way it had always done.
I saw the ground brown and sturdy under me
Always ready to reflect my leaning shadow.
I saw the grey round rocks on that ground;
They made crisp outlines against it.
And in the clearness of my vision
I realized, on this very episode of death,
That the child who first saw these things
Has not forgotten;
That these things have not moved since then;
That the affairs apart from these very basic things
Were a nothingness, a whirlwind, and a dissolution.

I am the observer of myself. I am the observer of nature, which shares with me the mysteries of which I myself am a part. I say to myself: Hope some. But if the object of hope does not approach my view, then let sorrow be of little importance, for the sorrow is enough with the meaning of life. A temporary relief at the sight of a friendly animal cannot be the same exhilaration that would come to its creator. A fleeting joy is apt to appease only slightly, while the consuming joy that would come with the Unchanging is unlikely to be known by me, now or later.

My philosophy, my tapestry of woven thoughts, is bent upon self-preservation. I suffer; I choose this philosophy. Always I have rejected the things I cannot use, everything that leads me away from the contemplation of meaning in pictures remembered.

Dorothy Thurston grew up in populated areas around New York City, Atlanta, Indianapolis, and in New Jersey. In 1961, she earned a B.F.A. degree in fine arts from the University of Iowa. She was group worker in art and writing for the N.Y.C. Department of Welfare and oil painting teacher for the Concord, New Hampshire, parks and recreation facility. While engaged in postgraduate studies in journalism at the University of Montana, she wrote public relations articles for the university. She wrote feature articles for periodicals and was copy editor for *Chicago Sun-Times/ Chicago Daily News.* In addition, she sought jobs she deemed fundamental: apple packer, potato gatherer, and caretaker of the sick and aged.

Woods have always been in her thoughts. She joins the spirit of nineteenth-century naturalist Henry David Thoreau who regarded nature as a way to peace and integration. She considers *Mt. Hersey Road* to be her principal artwork.